Anonymous

**The Irish Peasant**

A Sociological study

Anonymous

**The Irish Peasant**
*A Sociological study*

ISBN/EAN: 9783744717984

Printed in Europe, USA, Canada, Australia, Japan

Cover: Foto ©Suzi / pixelio.de

More available books at **www.hansebooks.com**

# THE IRISH PEASANT

## 𝔄 Sociological Study

*EDITED FROM ORIGINAL PAPERS*

BY

## A GUARDIAN OF THE POOR

LONDON: SWAN SONNENSCHEIN & CO.

NEW YORK: CHARLES SCRIBNER'S SONS

1892

# PREFACE.

In the following pages are to be found the personal experiences of one who led the life herein described. There are few persons in whom the spirit of inquiry is so strong as to suffer much hardship in order to get to the bottom of a commonplace subject. This, it may be truthfully stated, has been done. Perhaps it may furthermore be found that the subject is not so commonplace as it seems at first sight. Much that is unknown, or little known by the world at large, is to be found in these pages, so that in one sense, at least, they will not be commonplace. And in another sense they will be found somewhat uncommon, in that they contain the results of the observations of a man of unbiased views. He was a real person, anxious only to discover the truth as to a matter in which he felt a deep interest. Indeed, its truthfulness and freedom from prejudice must form the editor's best excuse for the publication of this autobiography.

The book also contains some useful information about matters of present public interest. For such there is a great need just now; party spirit runs high, and few writers or speakers can be looked on as being unprejudiced. Whatever the shortcomings of this part of the book may be, it is at least written in an impartial spirit. It may be added that the facts and figures are from the best sources, and are capable of proof.

THE EDITOR.

# CONTENTS

CHAP.                                                                         PAGE

I. INTRODUCTORY - - - - - - - I

II. RACES WHICH HAVE SETTLED IN IRELAND - - 20

III. THE RURAL ECONOMY OF ULSTER - - - 37

IV. THE RESOURCES OF THE PEOPLE - - - - 54

V. LOCAL GOVERNMENT - - - - - - 68

VI. IRISH ESTATES AND THEIR INHABITANTS - - 82

VII. THE IRISH LABOURER - - - - - - 103

VIII. IRISH EDUCATION - - - - - - - 119

CONCLUSION - - - - - - - 133

APPENDIX - - - - - - - 149

# THE IRISH PEASANT.

## CHAPTER I.

### INTRODUCTORY.

I WAS born in London, where my father had a house in an old-fashioned and highly respectable square. In due course, I was sent to that ancient university which has turned out so many great divines, states-men, and men of thought. At the university, I took part in most movements of the day, particularly in those of a philosophical nature, and, having taken a respectable degree, returned to my home. I was not long there until my father died. This was a heavy blow. My mother had long gone before, and I had neither brother nor sister. I was quite alone in the world, and free to do as I liked. My father had been a man of considerable property, all of which had been left to me; part of it was in Ireland, a country in which my mother had been born. I felt puzzled to know where to turn. I could not live on in the gloomy, old house alone. But whither should I go? Suddenly the thought struck me, "Why not go to

A

Ireland ? " it is a beautiful country, now much talked of, and a great field for the friend of progress. I soon acted on my idea, let my house for a term of years, and sailed for Ireland.

After a voyage of several hours in a steamer, I landed at a little seaport on the shores of an Irish loch. Black, savage-looking mountains rose straight from the sea on either hand ; their lower slopes were cut up into small patches of tillage, and trees seemed to be unknown. Altogether, the scene was gloomy and depressing. In order to see the shores of the loch, I took a passage in a small steamer which went from the port at which I had landed to a larger town at the head of the bay or loch. I had a full view of either side as we steamed slowly along ; one place in particular seemed strange to me who had never before seen such things. This was a mountain-side covered from top to bottom with small houses or huts, dotted over it like a flock of seagulls. The hillside was cut up into small patches of cultivation which ran nearly to the summit. I asked the steamboat skipper how these people lived : he told me that they were nearly all hawkers, pedlars, and fish-men or fish-women. Some had a donkey and cart, and vended herrings and cockles far and near. Others, who had no donkey, carried baskets and sold, some lemons, some apples, some fish, just as these things were in season. Children began their lessons in hawking by " taking out a few lemons in a net." For the hut and "bit of ground " a trifling rent was paid, and it was useful as a home to return to, or as a shelter in old age. How the land in such bleak, cold regions could be worth working, or be made grow anything, puzzled me.

I was landed at a little village, whence I hired a jaunting car, on which I drove to the small watering-place at which my father used to stay when he visited Ireland. It was a little town or village on the other side of the mountain range I had crossed, and on the open coast. The town was commonplace, being made up of whitewashed houses and cottages, plain and ugly, but slated and neat. Everything was modern. It seemed that at one time there had been nothing but thatched hovels, and a few of these yet stood at one end of the village. I stayed the night at a little inn, having ordered a car to be ready in the morning for a long drive. I intended the first thing to call on a Mr. M'Whirter, whom I had heard my father speak of as a man of great sense and shrewdness. I wanted to advise with him both as to finding a residence, there not being one on my estate, and as to some improvements I intended to make.

On a fine morning in early summer, I started for Mr. M'Whirter's house, which was some twenty-five miles off. At first I drove through a flat country, bare and ugly, ragged, furze fences divided the fields from one another, and long, low, thatched houses were dotted here and there over the country. These houses seemed to be comfortable, and the land looked fertile, and bore good crops of flax, oats, potatoes, and wheat. Having driven for a few miles through this flat district, the country began to rise, and instead of furze ditches were dry stone walls, and the houses were better, many of them being slated. Again the scene

changed and I came out on a dismal-looking, upland
tract. Here, black-looking hovels stood forth against
the sky in hideous nakedness. Drains and pools filled
with black and slimy water lay along the road, which
was carried at some height above the surrounding
country. Road and country had once been on a level,
but the peat had all been cut away, save the narrow
strip along which the road was carried. Such places
as these are very common; no effort seems to be
made to improve them; wretched beings squat there
and try to make a living by selling the few remaining
peats they can cut, and trying to grow a few potatoes
in the "spent moss," or cut-away bog. All this dreary
tract, together with miles of craggy hills, covered
with poor tenants, belonged to the Earl of Blunderbore, a great absentee landlord. His land was said
not to be dear, but between its sterility and the way
in which it was subdivided, it seemed to be impossible
to make a living on it at any terms. After driving
for many miles through this miserable district, we at
length came into a fertile-looking country, where
there were some large farms and good houses. The
driver, pointing to the best of these, said that it was
Mr. M'Whirter's, who, it seemed, was farmer, miller,
and cattle-dealer, all in one.

Accordingly, we drove up a little avenue to the
door of Mr. M'Whirter's house. It was a stylish,
villa-like abode, well plastered and finished. I pulled
a bell handle several times, but no one came to the
door. At last, after about half-an-hour, the door,
creaking on its rusty hinges, was pushed open about
a foot or so, and the frowzy, yellow head of a servant

wench was thrust forth. She crossly asked what I wanted. I replied that I wanted to see the master; she then asked me why I could not go to the back door like "any other body." I suppose that I must have looked astonished, for she burst out laughing, so did the car-driver. I then found out that gentlemen like M'Whirter built their houses for show, and not for use. A good house was merely an index or proof that its owner had risen in the world. The old dwelling was left standing joined to the new one at the rear, and in it the master dwelt. The new house was only used on rare, state occasions, when some display was thought to be needful. The front door having been opened with some difficulty, I was shown into a damp room, gaudily furnished. In a few minutes, Mr. M'Whirter came into the room. He was a powerfully built man, with a large, coarse mouth, and small, cunning eyes. His manner was friendly, but not over-polite; he seemed in some way to look down on me. I explained to him my reasons for coming to Ireland, said that I wanted a residence, and wished to carry out improvements and benefit the people. He listened with a pitying smile, and asked me if I wanted his opinion. I replied that I should be glad to have it. "Well, then," said he, "my dacent man, I'll tell you what it is; if you'll be guided by me, ye'll just take yourself off by the next boat that sails, and never show your nose here again. And I'll give you some more advice, too, but first we must have something to drink." Having ordered in a decanter of whisky, a jug of water, and some glasses, he poured me out about half a tumbler of whisky, and pressed me to drink. Now, I should not have objected to something to eat, but to drink spirits in the daytime, without eating, was contrary to my habits. However, I just raised the glass to my lips and set it down again; this inability to drink spirits seemed to sink me yet lower in M'Whirter's esteem. "Now," said M'Whirter, "I must be quick, I have to be in the mill and have no time to lose. As I was saying, either go back to where you came from, or else, if you do want to live over here, rent a farm on the Blunderbore estate. What would you be doing with a gentleman's residence? Drive your trap, and drink your glass, take off your hat to the agent, and let all your schemes alone."

"But," said I, "I have always been treated as a gentleman, and besides, why should a man with four or five square miles of property settle down as a tenant farmer, and doff his hat to a land agent? Should I not have some standing and influence?"

"Is it you," said M'Whirter, with huge scorn, "you're not the style of man for that sort of thing. Now, there's Captain O'Shun-the-Battle, the Blunderbore's agent, there's a man to carry weight anywhere.[1] A lofty, high-minded, military, or, at least, militiaman, wears no end of jewellery, drinks champagne and whisky every day, and the roar of his voice would make you shake in your shoes. What are you with your plain dress and quiet voice beside a man like that? Just nowhere! Why, none of the quality here would have anything to do with you. Or there's M'Swagger, the spinning-mill manager, a yet greater

[1] All real characters, and literally true.

man than O'Shun-the-Battle. That's what you may call a real gentleman, and a high Conservative as well. He's bought a place here that belonged to the Fitzmaurices, a wheen of auld, Popish rats, dating from the times of Strongbow. He's levelled the old castle, built a big new house, well plastered, and with plate-glass windows from top to bottom, where the castle stood, and cleared away every scrap of old work about the place. Broke 'em up, indeed, and bottomed the new avenue with them, the right way to serve them."

"Surely," said I, "you don't call a man like that a Conservative?"

"Don't I, indeed," said M'Whirter. "Why, do you know what he did last election? He drove five electors up to the poll in a four-horse brake, wi' an orange flag flyin', and a horn blowin', and every one of these men was so drunk when he came back that he had to be lifted out of the brake. Ah," said my friend, with an air of relish, "that's a real gentle-man, and is out and out the finest man in the county."

It was quite plain that M'Whirter's views and mine disagreed on everything. It seemed useless to stop longer, so I took my leave, mounted my car, and slowly and sadly drove back to my inn, which I did not reach till late at night.[1]

Next day, I made every possible inquiry about renting a house, but could hear of nothing. I then drove to my estate, which I had not as yet seen. It was in a rough, unimproved part of the country, but

[1] See appendix A.

the farms were of a good size and the houses slated mostly. My father had been careful to check sub-division, and to have houses well roofed. My first visit was at the house of an old man, who after eyeing me curiously, said, " You've fine times of it, landlord, drivin' about." This remark struck me as something new. The people seemed to grudge that anyone should be better off than themselves. I afterwards found that this feeling was quite common. All my tenants seemed to look on me with suspicion and dislike, and I was about as popular a person as a tax-collector. They had nothing to complain of, but a person who wanted rent or money in any form from them could not be otherwise than odious. The steward or bailiff, who was the most civil person I had met with, told me of a man who wished to sell his interest in a cottage, which had been built on the site of an old residence on the property. It then occurred to me that as I could get nothing better, perhaps my best way would be to buy this man's interest and settle down on my own property. I might as well do that as take M'Whirter's advice and be a tenant under the Blunderbore agent, and besides, I might win the con-fidence of my tenants by living like one of themselves. Having made up my mind to take this course, I went at once to look at the cottage, which I found to be stone-built and slated, having two rooms and a kitchen. We soon struck a bargain with the tenant who had been abroad and wanted to go back. He agreed to clear out at once, and I agreed to take over all furniture and fixtures. These consisted of a table and a few chairs made of beechwood, a bedstead, and bedding, and a few cooking utensils. The owner of these was a bachelor, who had roughed it in back settlements abroad, and his habits were simple. As the few unmarried peasants had old women to keep house for them, I hired a clean, decent-looking old peasant woman, who could bake oatcake and cook a bit of bacon. This was the staple diet of the people, varied by a few potatoes, and on state occasions white bread and tea. Few lived on better fare, almost nobody on worse. I made up my mind to live as the average peasant did, also to walk instead of riding or driving. I could not then be sneered at as being "better than other folks." There were thirty or forty acres of land attached to the house; this I determined to keep in my own hands and manage myself.

In a few days I moved into the cottage. At first I found my life a hard one, and wearied of the coarse diet. But it was that of nearly everyone about. In the course of a few days I had been in every farmhouse and cottage on my estate, and had found the fare to be nearly alike in all.

Seeing the great need of fences, I hired a country mason to build up the worst places, particularly those by the roadside. This was interesting kind of work. The walls were built of dry stones, and a little mortar was used in coping them. I took daily lessons in this work, to the scorn of all passers-by, who sometimes stood and spoke half-pityingly, half-scoffingly. These walls were well spoken of by the tenantry, as they kept cattle from straying, and saved the cost of " herding " them. At first the mason did not like my helping him; I was finding out too much; but as I

saved him the cost of a man to attend him and gave
him his own price for his work, he bore with me.    I
found the out-door life agree with me: I grew healthier
and had a better appetite for my coarse fare ; I slept
soundly and felt better in every way than I had done
since my boyhood.

Wall-building was work for summer.   At other
seasons of the year, I spent my time either tending
a little flock of sheep which I kept on my farm, or in
rambling about my property and the surrounding
country.   I was bent on mastering the Irish problem,
and determined to discover all that could be seen or
known in every direction.   In the course of two or
three years, I had gained a fair knowledge of the
rural economy of my own neighbourhood and of some
thirty miles round about.   Coarse attire, rough work-
ing-man's hands, and the best attempt I could make
at speaking the dialect of the country, all these helped
me greatly in my investigations.

Having quite exhausted my own part of the world,
I thought of travelling farther afield, in fact of walking across Ireland from its eastern to its Atlantic
coast.   I had now mastered to some extent the difficulty of Irish dialects, having had good opportunities
of learning them.   The country round was mixed as to
its population, and dialects varied from broad Scotch
to the usual Irish sort of talk spoken with a slight
northern accent.

One morning about the end of spring or beginning
of summer, I set out on my travels, in the character
of a mason.   I was clad in a coarse suit of country-
made tweed, on my feet were hobnailed brogues, and

my luggage was contained in a coloured handkerchief slung at the end of a stout walking-stick. My first night was passed in a travellers' lodging in a village some twenty-five miles from home. "Lodgings for Travellers" in Ireland are in a cottage or cabin in a village street. Outside is posted up a notice, "lodgings and entertainment." "Entertainment" means board. Sometimes the notice runs good "dry" lodgings— "dry," here means without board. The accommodation at such places is usually very poor. The beds are generally of straw stuffed into sacks or mattresses, the bedding coarse and dirty, and the food bad. Of course prices are low, the class of persons who travel on foot in Ireland being very poor. They are for the most part beggars, tinkers, navvies, tradesmen out of work, and tramps of different sorts. The aristocracy of these classes who can afford to pay for bed and board stay at lodgings, those who can't afford this luxury put up at the casual ward of the workhouse.

I started from my lodgings very early, and walked all that day. As I got towards the central parts of Ireland, the appearance of the country began to alter. Neat farmhouses and good cultivation became fewer and less. Bogs[1] and cabins became more and more plentiful. From the bogs rose low hills, covered with bright green grass, on which large cattle lazily fed. By the roadsides were grimy looking cabins, the thatch green with slime and moss, the walls black from age and smoke. The climate had become much damper, and the atmosphere reeked with moisture

[1] See appendix B.

and peat smoke. Towards nightfall, I stopped at a
cabin to ask my way to the nearest village. The
woman of the house asked me to come in, and set a
chair for me before the fire, beside which the owner
of the house was already seated, smoking a short
black pipe. There was no lack of fuel, and the fire
was heaped with peats—here called sods of turf—and
over the fire a big pot of potatoes hung from an iron
hook. The master of the house and I soon became
friends ; my horny hands and coarse dress showed
that I was "one of the people," and there was no
reserve or suspicion on my host's part. He showed
me two cows, which were tied up in one end of the
cabin, separated from the apartment in which we
were seated by a mud partition. I now had learnt
enough about cattle to know that they were good,
useful animals, in by no means bad order. During
the daytime they grazed along the roadsides or on
patches of herbage among the marshes, at night they
got a little coarse hay.

I was now about to leave the cabin and walk on to
the next village, but such a thing was not to be heard
of—I must stay the night. To this I at once agreed,
being curious to know more of the way of living of
these people. After a few minutes the pot which
hung over the fire was unhooked, the water poured
off, and a heap of dry floury potatoes turned out on
the table. Each person being supplied with a tin
porringer of milk, we began our supper. The meal
over, we drew our rush-bottomed chairs to the fire,
and smoked and talked. My host smoked the tradi-
tional Irish pipe. This is now greatly out of date, so

that an account of it may be of interest.  This pipe is about two inches in length, and of a dark brown or black hue from age and use.  The proper method of filling it is to pack and well press down the tobacco. This is cut from a stick or twist, which has been well soaked with oil to make it heavy and sell well—so at least the country folk say.  There are various ways of lighting the pipe.  The old-fashioned way was by a flint and steel, the down of a thistle being sometimes used as tinder.  The most common way, perhaps, is by holding a lighted sod of turf to the bowl of the pipe.  But of late years lucifer matches have come greatly into fashion.  Lighting the pipe is by no means easy, but, once " started," it does not easily go out.  When the pipe is going, the smoker sends forth a puff every one or two minutes, and talks in the intervals between each whiff.  The pipe is looked on as a great means of quickening conversation and strengthening friendship.

My host's discourse was practical; he cared little for theorising, and still less for sentiment. He complained of good land being all let to big graziers, and of " poor men " getting nothing but the bad bits that the others did not want, and " of prosecutions for grazing on the roadside." This was something new to me.  I had always heard of English lanes being let for the summer grazing by the local authority.  But it seemed that in Ireland people could not graze stock by the roadside on any terms, though they were quite willing to pay for the privilege.  Cow, donkey, or goat are forbidden to graze by the roadside, and must " move on," smart policemen having usually a string of such prosecutions at petty sessions.

The sharp little Irish boy or girl who mind the animals keep a good look-out for the " peeler," and when he is sighted in the distance, the animals are driven along the road. Sometimes the policeman suddenly appears from round a corner, and then the offenders are caught. This law seemed to bear very hardly on poor folk in Ireland, when it is taken into account that there is much more traffic on English lanes and roads than on those in Ireland. In most parts of Ireland there is almost no traffic on the country roads, and the danger arising thereto from animals grazing on the roadside must be very small. These were my host's chief grievances, and he seemed to have good grounds for his discontent. He cared little for politics. A law that would give him a bit of good ground cheap was all he wanted.

Having passed the night on some dried rushes covered with a spare blanket, and breakfasted on the same fare as that on which I had supped, I rose to depart. I wanted to pay something, but the man refused with a look of hurt dignity. He, however, accepted a little tobacco as an offering of friendship. Like many Irish peasants, he was hard and matter-of-fact, yet polite and hospitable. I have described this household because it was a fair type of many others in this part of Ireland. For some days I travelled through a country that seemed to consist of bogs, grazing tracts without habitations, save occasional mud cabins, and poor gravelly ridges of hills, swarming with small peasant holdings. I rambled for some

distance to the southward, and then turned north-
west. Having travelled in this direction for a few
days, I came into a mountainous region. There were
nothing but black, boggy-looking mountains, with
poor valleys lying between. Having followed the
course of a river, I at last reached the head of a bay
or loch. Here was a little town whose main street
was filled with emigrants, who had come in from the
country, and were going on to a seaport, whence they
were to embark for "foreign parts." These people
were nearly all young men and women, with a
sprinkling of married women and children, who were
going to husbands and fathers abroad. Their miserable attire seemed ill-suited for a sea voyage. But
with most of the peasantry shoddy and cheap finery
had supplanted the warm frieze and woollens formerly worn. English people are apt to think that
the Irish are always in rags. I cannot say that I
have seen many rags in Ireland. But English-made
clothes of the vilest shoddy are far too common.
These are sold in Irish fairs by dealers in such things.
They look cheap for the price asked, and so tempt ignorant young men and lads. Female attire of an equally
flimsy and worthless character is sold by the village
shopkeepers. I have often thought that many English manufacturers of so-called cheap stuffs must profit
well from the folly of young Irish men and women.
In out-of-the-way places frieze and coarse cloth of
home manufacture are yet worn by the men, and blue
cloth cloaks by the older women, and of late years
efforts have been made to extend the manufacture of
Irish woollens. But they are unable to keep pace

with cheap English shoddies, and many people in
Ireland think that protective duties ought to be levied
on such fabrics.[1]

I stayed the night at this town and in the morning
took a road that led along the shores of the loch.
Great dark mountains rose on the opposite coast sheer
from the water's edge. Everything was on a large
scale, unless the huts of the people, here of the
smallest size I had yet seen. They were built of
large stones and thatched with heather, tied down by
straw ropes, crossed and re-crossed. All day I walked
by these gloomy shores, and towards nightfall came
to a house to which I had been directed in the town
I had left. It was a small, slated farmhouse, where
lodgings were let to country-folk, who came to the
" water," as the seaside is called in Ireland. Here I
made an arrangement with the owner to work at
drystone walls at such times that the weather allowed,
or as suited my convenience, the work done to count
for so much in my bill for board and lodging. I
arranged to stay during the summer, and bargained
that on those fine days on which I wished to make
expeditions I should not be required to work. I
thought it better to keep up the character of working-
man, in order that I might be the better able to get
to the bottom of things.

Accordingly, next morning I set out for a walk to
the mouth of the loch. The little farmhouse was a
few miles from this opening, and the road to the open
coast wound up a steep mountain-side. When I got to
the top of this mountain, the other side descended as

---

[1] See appendix C.

a cliff down into the open Atlantic. The view here was a splendid one. The mouth of the loch must have been several miles in width. On either side, especially on the farthermost from me, arose steeply great promontories or heads with cliff-like faces. Against these thundered the huge Atlantic seas, rolling down from the Arctic regions without a check. It was a cloudy day with a strong north-west wind and gleams of sunshine now and then. The sun shone on the great white-crested waves, the spray from which flew far up the steep, black faces of the rugged head-lands. Thousands of sea-birds of all sorts were flying around, or sitting ranged in rows on the rocks waiting for the tide to ebb. The whole scene was such as I had never before witnessed; wildness, majesty, and a sort of rugged beauty seemed striving for the mastery.

I spent the summer, working and rambling over the country by turns. Sometimes I spent two or three days from home, particularly on one occasion on which I travelled out to the far western coast, as had been my intention to do at first. Here, as I sat on a big stone by the gloomy ocean, I summed up in my mind all I had seen and heard during my trip from the farmhouse to the western shore. The dismal tales of famine and distress I had heard among the people through whom I had travelled occurred to my mind and weighed down my spirits. Things looked bad enough, but the people seemed to try to make them worse, and to gloat over their own misery. What, indeed, could be done with such districts, hopelessly sterile, drenched by Atlantic rains, and crowded with starving people ?

I returned from this dismal region more quickly than I went, and felt thankful to find myself back again at the farmhouse.

Another trip I made to a sandy shore where people were busy gathering seaweed. It was a picturesque sight: men and women were loading panniers, slung across the backs of ponies and donkeys, with seaweed, which the big Atlantic seas, rolling in over the sands, left behind. These people all spoke Irish or Gaelic. One man, to whom I spoke, had "no English;" but he had manners and native politeness, for he offered me in dumb show two crabs, which he had caught among some rocks. He wanted nothing for them, nor did my appearance in working dress look like a "tip." I have always found that the more primitive and less civilised Irish were the best-mannered. The Irish who have been much in England or America are generally ill-mannered, often rude and offensive.

Another man who spoke some English asked me if I thought that the French were likely to come again to free Ireland. I wondered somewhat at the question, but found out afterwards that there had been a battle between some French and English frigates off this coast.

The boats used in these parts of Ireland seemed curious to one who had never seen them before. They were called "curraghs" or "corachs," and were canoes formed by stretching tarred canvas over barrel hoops. They were sharp at either end and a transverse section would be nearly semicircular. The oars were very narrow bladed and worked on a pin, something after the fashion of those on the north-east coast of England.

There is little more to describe about this neighbourhood. The people, though not in so miserable a state as in some places, were yet very hostile to those above them, both landlords and government coming in for their share of popular hatred. The landlords were an absentee nobleman, and a flax-spinner, who had made money and bought land. They were represented by agents, who screwed what rent they could from the people, and by keepers who prosecuted for killing rabbits. The State was represented by the armed police, who spent most of their time "still hunting," *i.e.*, searching out unlawful or unlicensed distillers of whisky. For this offence the penalty was high, yet stills were common, particularly in wet seasons, when unmarketable oats were used for making spirits or "poteen."

At the end of the summer I returned to my own house, having largely added to my stock of experience. That winter and the next summer I spent in further travelling over Ireland, chiefly across the country in south-westerly and westerly directions. The country seemed to repeat itself very much, bogs and rich grazing tracts in the central parts of the island, and mountains on the coast.

# CHAPTER II.

## RACES WHICH HAVE SETTLED IN IRELAND.

I HAD now become tired of travelling. I had found out
and investigated nearly everything of any interest. I
had gone about in different characters, and got together a mass of facts of different sorts. At the beginning of another winter I thought that I could
not spend my evenings better than in sorting and
arranging these facts, drawing up brief collections
under their proper headings, which might afterwards be of use either to myself or to someone else.

One of the first discoveries I made after coming to
Ireland was that, as a rule, difference of religion
meant also difference of race. I found two races
living side by side, but known from each other by
religious not racial names. This is an extraordinary
state of things, nowhere else found in the British
Isles. In order to account for it, a brief history of the
settlements in Ireland becomes necessary.

As everyone knows, the original inhabitants of
Ireland were Celts, or persons of Celtic blood. From
time to time the Danes conquered and settled in parts
of the eastern and north-eastern coasts of Ireland.
There was a large Danish colony in Dublin, Christ
Church being the cathedral of the Danish bishop,
within the city walls. [1] The Danes and Irish waged

[1] The Bishops of Dublin and Waterford received their con-

continued war against each other, the Danish power being finally overthrown at the battle of Clontarf. All along the coast both north and south from Dublin were strong Danish colonies. Waterford, Carlingford, Strangford, all Danish or Norwegian settlements, ford being a contracting or anglicisation of the Norse word "fiord." All these places are remarkable for being situated on narrow arms of the sea.

After the Danes came the Normans, who landed with Earl Strongbow in the reign of Henry II. They settled in different parts of Ireland, but chiefly in the east. Many settled at Waterford, more were scattered through the country, but the chief Norman colonies were near Dublin and in Lecale, a part of Ulster. John de Courcy, with several followers, sailed along the coast northwards from Dublin until they came to Lecale. This is often called Isle Lecale, and is a sort of peninsula running out into the Irish sea from west to east. On its western side are marshes which at one time must have been impassable, on every other side is the sea, hence the term Isle Lecale. Sailing northwards from Dublin and keeping the coast well in view, as was then the custom, the southern coast of Lecale would lie right ahead, and be the first land the voyagers would meet with. John de Courcy and his men were no doubt glad to take possession of Lecale, which is a fertile district free from waste, and sloping to the south. The well-armed Normans must have

secrations from Canterbury, and had nothing to say to the Irish Church. This state of things was changed after the overthrow of the Danes.

had little difficulty in driving the native inhabitants to the mountains. However, they do not seem to have despised their foes, for De Courcy built a number of castles along the shore of his newly conquered territory. The Norman-English seem to have altogether taken possession of this district, and to have driven out all, or nearly all, of the ancient inhabitants. At the present day most of the Lecale names are of Norman origin. Such names as Lascelles, Fitzsimon, Denver, from D'Anvers, are quite common among peasants and fishermen.

This colony seems to have continued un-Irish for a long time after its settlement. Centuries after its conquest, while the people of Ardglass were at mass in the parish church, it was surrounded by a body of native Irish. The church was set on fire, and those of the congregation who tried to escape were speared by the native Irish. After this the Ardglass people had to build their church within the fortifications of the town.[1] This might be looked on as a proof that Irish animosities are racial rather than religious, for both Norman-English and native Irish at this time professed the same religion. But the number of castles found here is a proof of the state of constant warfare in which both races lived.

By degrees the Anglo-Normans pushed northwards from Lecale and took possession of a district afterwards called White's country; and most of the peninsula of Ards came to be owned by Roland Savage, an Anglo-Norman. There were also Norman-English settlements south of Lecale at Greencastle and Car-

---

[1] *Ecclesiastical Antiquities,* by Dr. Reeves, Bp., Down,

lingford. At the latter place are yet the ruins of a magnificent castle called King John's Castle, and nearly opposite is Greencastle, a square Norman keep.

Near Larne, far north of Lecale, was a small Norman colony, and the remains of a castle may still be found.[1]

The Norman-English settlement near Dublin was perhaps the largest in Ireland. Many Norman names may now be found near the metropolis.

Lunders, a common Dublin name, is said to come from De Loundres, and there was an archbishop of that name in the twelfth century. Fitzgerald, Fitzsimon, Fitzmaurice are quite common names in eastern Ireland.

At Waterford, the name Power is very common. This name comes from the Norman De La Poer.

If the number and commonness of Norman names are any proof, there must be a very great infusion of that blood among the people of eastern Ireland. Whether this fact accounts in any way for the high military qualities displayed by many Irishmen is at least an open question.

Of course Norman-French names must be carefully distinguished from Huguenot-French names, as there were small settlements of the latter, in Dublin and parts of Ulster and Leinster. These Huguenot names are to be found chiefly among the mercantile classes in Dublin and Ulster. De La Touche is the name of a respectable old banking firm in Dublin. And the linen trade of Ulster is greatly indebted to a M. Crommelin, descendants of whom may yet be found in the north of Ireland. These Huguenot colonists, if indeed they may be called so, were few in number

---

[1] See appendix D.

and confined very much to one class. They cannot be said to have had much, if any, influence on the body of the people. The Huguenots are mentioned here rather out of their proper place, as they were the latest body of settlers in Ireland. But as their names might be confounded with Norman-French names, it has been thought best here to distinguish between the two.

From the reign of Henry II. to the end of that of Elizabeth there were no settlements of any note in Ireland. But about the end of the sixteenth century an English colony, headed by Sir Arthur Chichester, settled in part of Antrim. This was followed by some other small English colonies, and in the reign of James I. the settlement known as the "plantation of Ulster" took place. This story is known to every reader of English history. Suffice it here to state that the London companies, to whom the King made large grants of escheated estates, still hold their own for the greater part. But these estates were not chiefly settled by Englishmen, as might be supposed, but by lowland Scotchmen. Lowland Scotch names and the Presbyterian form of religion will now be found to prevail in this part of Ireland, the mountainous parts remaining in the hands of the descendants of the ancient Irish inhabitants. Many other grants were made, chiefly to Scotchmen, who brought a certain number of men with them to settle the country. In order to protect themselves from the wrath of the ancient inhabitants, who had been driven forth to make room for them, the colonists settled as much as possible in the same places. This led to certain districts being formed in which for several miles round no Irishman was to be found. The settlers were quite numerous enough to find wives in their own settlements, and hence, from that time to the present, they have kept up all their manners and traditions. This accounts for the fact of there being yet found in Ulster districts wholly Scotch in every way, save perhaps that they may have customs or idioms which have in modern Scotland died out.

The chiefs of these colonies, to whom grants of land were made on certain terms, were for the most part mere adventurers. The founder of one great family was a spy, who pretended to keep a school in Dublin in order to gain information. And many others were hungry hangers-on at the Court, whom the King wanted to get rid of. Though some of them bore good Scotch names, their descendants are unable to prove any connection with the great families from branches of which they claim to be descended.[1] This "plantation of Ulster" is the colony about which almost everyone knows something. But there was a later Scotch colony about which few persons know anything.

As is well known, in the struggle between Charles I. and the Parliament, the Irish chiefs took the King's side. This was the losing side, and the chiefs lost their lands. These were granted by Cromwell to all sorts of people, many of them very worthless characters. One very large estate, or rather territory, was granted

[1] See Burke. The descent is *stated* in many cases, but *not shown*.

to an English adventurer, whilst the rightful owner was said to have been "shut up in Kilkenny fighting for the King." This estate was in Ulster, and after the restoration the true owner was unable to get his property restored. He was the greatest instance, but there were many others as well. Some lands were restored, but Cromwell's confiscations had been on so wholesale a scale that it was deemed dangerous to meddle with all his grantees.

Now, if we turn to a survey of this time, large districts will be found in Eastern Ulster which had been completely devastated and laid waste by Cromwell in revenge for 1641. In surveys of the eighteenth century these districts are found to be well peopled by persons of Scotch names. It may be asked, when did they settle in these districts? To this inquiry it is not easy to reply. The facts seem to be that at first the wasted country was granted in large blocks to adventurers without any conditions as to colonisation being made, and that from time to time emigrants from Scotland settled on the best parts of these estates.[1] A large number of these seem to have arrived at the end of the seventeenth century, during the conflict between James II. and the Covenanters. Their descendants bear West of Scotland names, and there is still a small religious body in Ulster calling themselves Covenanters. I remember once talking to an old woman who said that she could trace her descent from the time of the "persecution" in Scotland, when her great-great-grandfather had come to Ireland. There being no scheme for State colonisation, and the

[1] See appendix E.

settlers having just crossed when and how they liked, may account for there being no public record of this settlement. In fact, it cannot be called a settlement—it was rather a gradual colonisation.

These Norman and Danish colonies of the twelfth and previous centuries, and the Scotch colonies of the seventeenth centuries, are the great settlements which have stamped their character on the people of Ireland down to the present. There have been several smaller settlements, such as those of the English and Huguenots already mentioned, the Cromwellian, and the Dutch of William III., together with the German palatines in the South of Ireland. None of these have left much impress behind them. Huguenot and Dutch names are to be found, but that is all. It would require a very fertile imagination to trace the likeness between any Irishman now to be found and Dutchmen. As to the Cromwellian settlement of Ireland, that is well-known matter of history. Although much Irish land was granted to Cromwell's followers, which for the most part they have been able to keep, their numbers, save in one part of Ireland, were few. This part of Ireland was Tipperary, and some parts of the adjoining counties. Here many of the people are said to be descended from Cromwell's soldiers and camp-followers and Irish women. To how great an extent this is true it would now be impossible to say. There is no doubt that there is some truth in the assertion. As to the present aspect of these people, they seem thoroughly Irish, profess the religion of the vanquished race, and their part of the Island is, to say the least of it, not the most peaceful,

One result of all these successive colonies was that
the ancient Irish and the old Anglo-Norman settlers
forgot their feuds, and combined together against the
new colonists.  In Ulster, the Anglo-Normans had, to
a certain extent, to yield to the new settlers, and their
northern settlements of Ard's and White's country
passed into Scotch hands.  Even part of the old
Norman colony of Lecale was settled by Scotchmen,
but to a very small extent.  There the Normans were
better able to hold their ground.

In Leinster the old English settlers suffered to a
much greater extent.  The lords of the English pale
and their followers had been chiefly on the side of
Charles I., and on the defeat of the royalists, lost
their property and were banished to Connaught.  To
readers of history is well known the choice offered by
Cromwell between Connaught and a place very much
hotter than that province.  In addition to those
banished to Connaught, were the people, women and
children chiefly, massacred at Drogheda, as well as
the numbers of royalists sent as slaves to the planta-
tions in the colonies.  In consequence of this blood-
thirsty policy, the level country round Dublin called
the pale, lost much of its English character and came
in after years to be greatly peopled from other parts
of Ireland.  Difference of religion, as well as greed to
possess their lands, caused all the new colonists, from
those of James I. to those of Cromwell, to hate the
old English settlers quite as much as the Irish.

No doubt after the Restoration some of the old
families were restored to their possessions, but many
were not, and these felt bitterly the seeming ingrati-

tude of the King to those who had lost all in his
father's service. One of the great reasons why so
many Irishmen fought for James II. was, the desire
on the part of the old English and ancient Irish to get
back the lands of which they had been despoiled.
Religion or personal attachment to James had little to
do with the matter.

This is the slightest possible sketch of the past.
It may serve to remind readers of history of the facts
which bear most on the present social aspect of
Ireland.

What, it may be asked, is now the position of these
settlers and the old Irish population? It is beyond all
question that in the seventeenth century a hard and
fast line was drawn between the settlers and native
Irish, or "Irishy" as they were called. And that
long after the reign of Henry II., the English of the
pale were quite another people from the "mere Irish."
Are all these jarring elements now fused into one race
as some would have us think, or do the old distinc-
tions yet survive? In these respects Leinster and
Ulster differ widely. In the former province and in
parts of Munster settled by the English, the colonists
have for the most part intermarried with the Irish,
and after a generation or two all difference seemed to
have been blotted out. Though the descendants of
these people have much in common with the Celts
they are not one with them. There may yet be ob-
served a marked difference between the people of
these mixed districts, and those in purely Celtic
localities. It is also a remarkable fact that the latest
settlers have fused much more with the native popula-

tion than have the earliest. The reason is that the
later settlers have come to parts of the country where
the Irish populations were overwhelming and soon absorbed the foreigners. But the infusion of Teutonic
blood was great enough to change the appearance and
nature of the old population to some extent. A new
race sprang up, large, and stolid in many ways, and
showing in form and feature the union of Celtic and
Teutonic blood. The Irish police force, particularly
the Dublin metropolitan police, are nearly all men of
this race.[1]

On the other hand the Danish and Anglo-Norman
colonies on the east coast, north of Dublin, having
settled in greater numbers, intermarried with each
other. The ancient Irish had been driven from the
plains of Fingal to the Wicklow mountains, whence
they constantly harried the Anglo-Irish of Dublin
and its neighbourhood. Some fields near Dublin, now
built over, were called the bloody fields, from the fact
of some Dublin citizens who were merrymaking there,
in the Middle Ages, being slain by the mountain Irish.
Even now if anyone is curious enough to go among
the people, say between Dublin and Drogheda, ask
their names and mark their appearance, and then go
among the people in the Wicklow mountains, he will
find a marked difference. In one district will be
found a large heavy people, bearing such names as
Sweetman, Smyth, Leonard, Lacy; in the other will
be found a people of lighter build and darker com-

[1] They are recruited largely from Tipperary and Queen's
County, parts of the country greatly settled by seventeenth
century English.

plexion, bearing such names as O'Toole and O'Byrne, great numbers of families bearing the same name.[1]

In the baronies of Forth and Bargy on the south coast of Wexford, also along the Wicklow coast, are many people of Welsh origin and bearing Welsh names, such as Buckley, Evans, Jones. These people are quite unlike the original inhabitants of those parts of Ireland.

In Ulster there has been but little fusion of the colonist with the native Irish. This is accounted for first, by the fact of the colonists settling in great numbers on large estates, and thus being numerous enough to marry among themselves; and next, from the bitterness of feeling on the part of the native Irish, who had been driven from their lands. The memories of the year 1641, when a great effort was made by the Irish to get rid of the intruders and regain possession of the forfeited lands, have much to do with the embittered race-hatred which yet prevails in Ulster. This was the last part of Ireland subdued by England, and the Celts at first, and afterwards the Celts and old English combined, stubbornly resisted to the very last the encroachments of the new settlers. As in Leinster, there is in Ulster a mixed race. There is a race descended from English pre-reformation settlers and pure Celts. These are usually quiet, well-conducted people. But there are also people descended from the later colonists and the old Irish,

---

[1] Lawrence O'Toole, Archbishop of Dublin, A.D. 1170, was of the Wicklow clan of O'Tooles. He was the last Archbishop of the old Celtic Church and race, his successors having been always Normans or Englishmen.

these are nearly always troublesome and ill-conducted. Fortunately for Ulster, this latter race, if it can be called such, is few in numbers. Suppose a line is drawn from east to west across Ulster from a point on the Antrim coast nearest Scotland to the western shore of Donegal. And further, suppose that a traveller follows this line. He will find at first, though but sixteen or seventeen miles from Scotland, a purely Irish people, in the glens of Antrim. Save that they speak with a northern accent, these people are as thoroughly Irish as those in almost any part of Ireland. Having passed up the glens and crossed the moorland, he will travel through a fertile and well-kept district, in which the people are Irish but in name. Here will be found Lowland Scotch names, Scotch dialect, and Protestant places of worship. This sort of country will continue for the most part along the northern coast of Ireland until Loch Foyle is crossed. In Innishowen will be found a Gaelic people, though, strange to say, considered by some persons to be less Celtic than the people of north Antrim, who are so near Scotland. Having crossed Loch Swilly, the country becomes more Celtic than that about Moville and through Innishowen, and when the western shore of Donegal is reached all traces of the colonists have disappeared.

All through this journey a hard and fast line is found to be drawn between Celt and Teuton. Even where scattered Protestant families are found in the Celtic districts, they are quite different from their neighbours. Of course, many Scotchmen are Celts, but the Scotchmen who have settled in Ireland are all

Teutons of Lowland origin. This may easily be known from their names. Nearly all Scotch names found in Ireland are either altogether Lowland, or names in both Lowlands and Highlands. A purely Highland name is a rare thing in northern Ireland.

Names of places will sometimes denote the race of people by whom a country was settled. This is partly the case in Ireland, but also to a very great extent not the case. Before going further with this subject it will be necessary to point out how Ireland is divided. Excepting ancient cities and municipal jurisdictions, Ireland is divided into townlands. This term comes from the Teutonic tun or ton, a boundary, and corresponds with the English ton. As Ireland was subdued by the English from time to time it was parcelled out into these townlands. A townland is of no particular size; some of them contain two hundred acres, others are two thousand acres in extent. They are of all sizes and forms. The " ton " is first met with in the old English pale, or level district around Dublin. Here the Irish names were disused, and the word "ton" or town with a name of thing or person prefixed substituted, e.g., Nuts-town, Old-town, New-town, Peirce-town, Joyce-town, Rowles-town, are names of places near Dublin. These names seem to show how thoroughly the country was settled by the English. In the plain the names of places are nearly always English, in the mountains to the south of Dublin names are Irish. In this part of Ireland where places have English names the people have, as a rule, English or Norman names. Where the people's names are Irish, the names of places are also Irish.

The reverse of all this is the case in Ulster. Here for some reason the ancient Irish names of places have continued to be used. Ballykelly, Ballymurphy, Listullycurran, Lisbane (or the White Fort), are all townlands peopled wholly by persons of Scotch blood, bearing lowland Scotch names.

In Southern and Western Ireland, both names of persons and names of places are for the most part Irish.[1]

The townland is the best known division in Ireland. A man's address is usually the townland in which his house or farm is situated. He may have his house in one townland and his farm in another. There may be many farms in a large townland, or a "big grazier" may hold several small townlands.

Parishes are the next largest ancient division after townlands. An Irish parish is generally much larger than an English one. It is a common thing to find in Ireland parishes ten and even twenty miles in length. Names of parishes in the English pale are sometimes anglicised, such as "Garristown" and "Monkstown," but as a rule the old Celtic names have been preserved. Why this should have been done in the case of parishes will probably be explained from the fact that the Norman-English found parishes and churches on their arrival, and saw no reason for meddling with their names. But when new divisions, such as townlands, were made, they naturally received English names.

The ancient parish is now disused as a division for public purposes. The Poor-Law electoral division has replaced it. This latter is more uniform in size, and on that account more convenient.

[1] See appendix F.

Baronies, which are the next largest divisions, correspond in some respects to English hundreds. A barony varies in size. Some baronies are twenty miles across, others not more than seven or eight miles in length. In Ulster the ancient names are used for both townland, parish, and barony. In the English pale some baronies, such as " Nethercross," are called by English names.

Irish counties are divided into these four divisions, *viz.*, townlands, parishes, Poor-Law electoral divisions, and baronies. Poor rates are levied for each electoral division, and not for the entire union. Highway rates, or, as they are called in Ireland, county cess, are levied for each barony. Both poor rates and county cess vary greatly, according to the nature of the division or barony.

As three of these divisions are historical, and connected more or less with the settlements in Ireland, this seemed to be the proper place to describe them.

Before concluding this chapter, one or two historical matters which have been lately brought forward by historians, as having some bearing on the present state of things, may be noticed. One is the long-forgotten story of 1641. This seems to have little bearing on the present condition of Irish society. Everything is now quite different. In the seventeenth century the Irish were a monarchical people, devoted to their chief and to their King. The movement of 1641 was led by the chieftains, in order to regain their ancient possessions, in the first place, and in the next it may have been a part of the great Civil War. It is a well-known fact that the bulk of the Protestant colonists were on the parliamentary side, and hostile to Charles I., whilst the Irish were devoted to his cause. The Irish are now a very democratic people, care nothing for the few remaining descendants of the ancient families, and are ready to join with people of any race or religion in getting what both may happen to want.

The other is a statement by an eminent historian,[1] to the effect that landlords evicted Protestant tenants, and supplied their places with those of another race and form of religion. There can be little doubt that this was done. During the war of American Independence some northern Irishmen fought against England.[2] And at the present day there are men of northern Irish descent in America who are very hostile to England. Doubtless there have been good reasons for all this hostility, and these may be found in the fact of these men's forefathers having been unjustly deprived of their farms. It is just possible, though, that the number of such cases may have been less than some persons are led to think. I have sought carefully throughout Ulster for proofs of this Celtic importation, and I have been able to find very few. Most of the Celts belonged to the old Ulster clans and had inhabited the same districts for centuries.

[1] Mr. Froude.          [2] *e.g.* Montgomery.

# CHAPTER III.

THERE exists much misunderstanding about this province. It no doubt differs in parts from any of the other provinces of Ireland, but in parts only; over its greater extent it is much like any of the other Irish provinces.

In fact the term "province" is altogether a misleading one. These divisions belong to very ancient history, and have no real meaning now. It so happens that the Scotch colonies are in Ulster, and that the north-eastern part of that province is chiefly inhabited by people professing the Protestant religion, that is all. However, it is much in one way, for it is enough to constitute a part of Ireland wholly unlike any other part. It has habits, manners, usages of its own, and requires a separate description, before any other part of Ireland is treated of.

By Ulster, here is meant those portions of counties in that province which have been settled in by English and Scotch colonists, chiefly the latter. Whatever may be said as to the fact of their having been settlements of English and French, there can be no doubt but that these have been altogether absorbed and swamped by the lowland Scotch element.

The customs of the settlers have spread to other dis-

37

tricts in the province, also to a slight extent their accent. In fact, Ulster may be divided, first, into districts wholly un-Irish; next, into districts Irish, but with some customs and habits of the settlers, such as tenant right and a slight northern accent; lastly, into districts completely Irish in every respect.

Ulster proper, that is the settlements, differs from other parts of Ireland in many respects. It is not proposed here to deal with all these aspects, which would require a large volume to do them justice. There are two or three more important things which it is needful to know something of, in order to form some general idea of the social condition of modern Ireland.

The first of these things is what is called the Ulster custom of tenant-right. It was an understood thing in the plantation of Ulster by James I. that every man settled on a forfeited estate should have a certain interest in the soil. Each built his own homestead, and naturally expected to have some interest or property in his own handiwork. He also drained and cleared the land, which, of course, in equity gave him an interest in the soil. These claims had merely the force of custom, they were never legally recognised. Ulster tenants bequeathed their farms, or sold them to other persons, always subject to the consent of the landlord. There was constant friction between the tenant and the landlord. The latter sometimes imposed a limited price, beyond which the farm should not be sold. Often he wanted to raise the rent, on a change of tenancy, and this was looked on by the tenant as an interference with his rights, and an injury to his interest in the soil. It was a kind of dual ownership and seemed never to have worked very smoothly.

On estates settled after the reign of James I., and where no custom or understanding existed, the tenant had in strictness no tenant-right. These districts were much larger than is commonly supposed, but the landlords would seem in course of time to have allowed a sort of tenant-right custom to grow up. They wished to amuse themselves or live in England, and a sort of tacit bargain was made with the tenantry that if they liked to build and improve, and ask nothing from the landlord, the latter would not disturb them; in short, that provided they paid a certain rent and voted for the landlord or his nominee, they might buy, sell, sub-divide, cut up, or do what they liked with the land. This was what it came to during the eighteenth and nineteenth centuries on what were called by a kind of satire, " good estates." Sub-division suited the landlord because it multiplied votes, and the custom of tenant-right always formed a sort of guarantee for the payment of the rent. If a man became unable to pay he could sell his interest, and the agent took good care to have all arrears paid out of the price of the tenant-right before he accepted the new tenant.

In course of time the estates settled under the plantation scheme of James I., and those settled at later dates, became much the same so far as tenant-right was in question. On both arose constant complaints from the tenants as to encroachments by the landlords, chiefly by limiting the price of

farms, and by raising rents on sales. It is one of the
most curious things about the history of this custom
that on what were called "bad estates," the tenants
were often the best. This arose from the fact that
"bad estates" being more sharply looked after, subdivision was checked, and the price of tenant-right
being limited, the tenant had more money left wherewith to work his farm.

On the "good estates," where sub-division was
allowed, and the tenant could sell his farm for whatever price he could obtain, farms sold for high prices.
For these reasons chiefly, first, because the farm being
small, it was within the means of a great many people
to bid for it; next, because there was no restriction
on the bidding; and, lastly, because the character of
the "office" or estate was good, and the rent was not
likely to be raised. As times grew better, prices of
land went up, twenty and thirty pounds per statute or
English acre being a common price for land rented
from year to year. It soon became impossible for
would-be tenants to find these sums, and then arose
one of the unmixed evils of the system—*i.e.*, borrowing money to buy farms. This money might be borrowed in different ways. It might be borrowed from
a friend or relative, or from a person who made
money-lending his business. Before sale of tenant-
right was legalised under recent statutes, it was
always a risky thing to lend money to buy farms
with. The landlord, though he could not so far fly
in the face of public opinion as to refuse to recognise
tenant-right, might yet hinder the money-lender
greatly. If a lender of money sold up a man who

had borrowed money to buy his farm, the landlord might refuse to accept the buyer as tenant. As this might have been the highest bidder, and as this bid might not exceed the amount borrowed, the usurer might be a loser. Again, the landlord might raise the rent, and so injure the value of the tenant's, or rather of the money-lender's, interest. Or he might refuse to allow the farm to be sold for more than a certain sum, although rules such as this were easily evaded.

When tenant-right was legalised, and the tenant could do very much as he liked, the evils of the borrowing system became much greater. There was now a legal security, and it became much easier to borrow money. Formerly, only part could be had; now, the whole purchase-money could be got without difficulty.

These money-lenders were of different classes. They might be country shopkeepers, or rich peasants, or retired tradesmen who had saved money. The usual rate of interest was five per cent. I never heard of a less rate. Commonly, the farmer borrowed a part of the purchase-money, but often he borrowed all of it. When he went to live on his farm, he began to realise the fact that he was paying two rents—one to the landlord, and another to the money-lender in the form of interest, the latter payment being often the largest.

The farm being usually small, and the double rent high, the tenant in good times could barely exist, and in bad times failed. He was, as a rule, the only sufferer. The purchase-money yielded by the sale of the farm paid, or nearly paid, the usurer, and the buyer of the farm had to pay any arrears to the landlord or " office." Suppose land to be let at one pound the acre, and that the tenant-right sells for twenty pounds an acre—a common price—then five per cent. on the purchase-money just doubles the rent. And when land is let at fifteen shillings an acre, and sold for twenty pounds an acre, the interest on the purchase-money more than doubles the rent. These rents, and these prices, are quite common. It may here be mentioned that in Ireland there are three sorts of acres—the Irish acre, the English or statute acre, and the Scotch or Cunningham acre. The Irish acre is nearly double the statute acre, and the Cunningham acre is midway in size betwixt the two former.

The latter is peculiar to the north of Ireland, and even there is only known in certain places. When people in Ireland talk of acres, they nearly always mean Irish acres. Travellers, therefore, are apt to suppose the farms to be smaller, and the rents higher, than is really the case.

The tenantry having now an interest in land which can be proceeded against, they are able to get an amount of credit which in former days would have been impossible. In most northern towns and villages are a class of men who keep shops in which almost everything is sold. They have a licence to retail strong drink, and there is always a counter in the back of the shop where glasses and half-glasses of whisky can be had, as well as other sorts of liquor. Groceries, drapery goods, artificial manures, odds and ends of all sorts are to be had at these establishments, and credit is freely given to anyone who is thought to be "good for the amount." People who go into these places to drink are tempted to buy, and often run in debt to an amount not justified by their means. The profits of these shopkeepers and publicans combined are large, and few persons, who do not understand the facts of the case, would credit the quantity of property they accumulate. The people are often the bondserfs of usurers and shopkeepers to whom they owe money. Indebtedness is the curse of some of these large Ulster estates. The wish to "get on" and to *look* at least as good as their neighbours causes people to borrow and run into debt, hoping by extra sharpness and thriftiness to struggle out of their embarrassed state. They are sometimes able to gain the wished-for end, but far oftener they fail to do so.

Another great source of embarrassment is the custom of a peasant or farmer leaving his interest in the farm to one of his sons, subject to legacies and payments to other members of the family. This habit is a direct outcome of the Ulster custom, for elsewhere, until of late years, the farmer would have no interest to charge with payments. Where the tenant has to make these payments at once, which frequently happens, he is obliged sometimes to sell off some of his stock. From the effects of this enforced sale, he often never recovers. It is a difficult matter for a man who has no money to get cattle together, and without them he is unable to farm profitably. The victim of this custom has too often to end his days as a heavily-weighted drudge, often worse off than the man whom he employs,

It is a remarkable fact, that these difficulties and embarrassments nearly always are greatest under what are called " good landlords," *i.e.*, those who allowed sub-division, free sale, and who never raised the rent; in short, allowed the tenants to do just as they liked, sub-ject to the payment of a certain rent. The reason why the tenants on these estates are always the poorest may be found in the fact that moderate rents and freedom of sale are not enough to counterbalance the evil effects of subdivision and neglect. The fact of non-interference, which is the great merit claimed by these landlords, usually forms a good excuse for utterly neglecting their properties, helping the tenants in no respect, and spending every penny of their rents in England or abroad.

This is the bad side of the Ulster custom; it has a good side also. Any person coming from other dis-tricts of Ireland into Ulster proper must be struck by the great difference in the appearance of the houses and farming from those seen elsewhere. In these dis-tricts where tenant-right has been in full swing for two or three centuries, are to be found comfortable farm steadings, and good tillage. There is also a look of independence and progress about everything and everybody. The Ulster custom must be credited with all this. These improvements have all been made by the people themselves, the landlords have done noth-ing. And it certainly is not likely that the tenants would have built and drained and expended money and labour on their land unless they had some security for doing so.

This is virtually a system of dual ownership, and

this system is now legally enforced all over Ireland,
whether for good or for evil. Many high authorities
have condemned the dual system of ownership ; they
say that Ulster has prospered in spite of the custom,
and that it is better either for the landlord to make
all improvements as in England, or for the cultivator
to own his farm. Dual ownership has not worked
very well in Ireland, during the past ten years, and
public opinion on the whole seems to be in favour of
the Irish tenant becoming absolute owner of his farm.
The people of Ulster may be said generally to be in
favour of a system of compulsory land purchase by
the State, which would make the tenants owners of
their farms, subject to annual payments for a certain
number of years.

Farms in these Ulster settlements vary in size.
On some estates subdivision has been recklessly
carried out, and the farms often do not average more
than fifteen statute acres. Farms of this size do not
work well, they are at once too large and too small.
They are too large to allow of the tenant being in
any employment or working at a trade, and they
are too small to occupy the tenant fully. Such
farmers can keep but one horse, and are obliged to
borrow or hire another in spring to do their field work.
This is always found to be an unsatisfactory arrangement, and such tenants are behind-hand with their
work and late with their harvest, and this is a serious
matter in a wet and cold climate. They are usually
a struggling class of men, never out of difficulties,
and the first to feel failure of crops or loss of cattle.
The origin of holdings of this size is altogether

political. Until of late years, twelve pounds annual valuation was the amount of occupancy needful to confer a vote. Therefore the large owners, who wished for political influence, favoured subdivision to the extent of a twelve or fifteen pound valuation, which meant a farm of from fifteen to eighteen acres. In one instance, a farm of thirty acres was said to have been divided into two fifteen-acre holdings, by a man who left half his farm to each of his sons. One man started in the farmhouse, and the other fitted up one of the outhouses as a residence; they shared the other outhouses between them. How such an arrangement was likely to work may be easily imagined, yet it was said to have had the warm approval of the "office," or agent who wanted votes. On these kind of estates may often be found two houses in the same close or yard, and the farm buildings mixed up. People living in this way are constantly fighting with one another, and are nearly always bad tenants.

Even yet northern landlords preserve their political influence, hence this subdivision, by those who are reckless enough to sacrifice their estates to their personal vanity. This policy is quite peculiar to parts of Ulster. Over the greatest part of Ireland, landowners have long since lost all political influence, and are more bent on getting rid of the people than on increasing their number.

It is a happy thing for Ulster, that this system of management is limited to very few estates. On most properties settled by the colonists, the people have enough of land, and there is no desire for subdivision.

The system of farming carried out varies from that of other parts of Ireland in a few important respects. One of the first of these is flax-growing. Nearly all the flax grown in Ireland is produced in Ulster, a little is grown in other parts of Ireland, but the quantity is comparatively small. Flax is not so much grown now as in former times. It has been found to be an uncertain crop and to exhaust the land greatly. Were it not for the gambling element to be found in human nature everywhere, this crop would perhaps not be grown at all. It is very uncertain, sometimes it succeeds, oftener it fails. If it succeeds it pays the grower very well. If it fails it causes a heavy loss, as the seed is costly and the crop requires much weeding and labour. Yet it is grown, for though the crop on the whole may be a failure, it often succeeds in particular cases, and these sometimes where it has been carelessly cultivated. Its success depends on many seemingly trifling events, such as getting a shower at the proper time. Taking the average during a series of years, it is very questionable if this crop does much more than pay its way, the expenses of seed, labour, and scutching or dressing are so high. Farmers are beginning to find this out, for except in a very few districts where the soil is specially suited for flax, it is grown but in small quantities by good farmers.

It is very doubtful if the profits of flax-growing counterbalance the loss, often very great, arising from the damage done thereby to the Fisheries. In order to understand this, it becomes needful to explain the process of saving flax. The flax is first pulled up by the roots, and tied in bundles, it is then steeped in water for a certain time. After some of the tissue of the plant has rotted off in the water, the flax is taken out, spread on grass fields to dry, and when dried tied again in bundles; put up in shocks in the fields, and when dry enough, stacked, generally in the stackyard, whence it is led to the mill to be "scutched."

For the most part, the flax is steeped in "holes," or long, open drains a few feet in width, dug out for the purpose. These are filled, some time previous to the flax being steeped, with water from a spring or stream. When the water has been softened sufficiently by lying in the holes, the flax is put in, and after some time taken out. The water is now quite black and has the most offensive stench, so much so, that the smell arising from the flax taken out of it and spread out to dry, is almost unbearable to those unused to it. A small portion of this water leaking out of the dam at the end of a flax-hole flowing thence into a river or stream is enough to poison numbers of fish.

In order to save labour, these flax-dams or holes are nearly always made in the course of a small rivulet, so that some overflow or leakage is unavoidable. Sometimes they are made close to the banks of a larger stream, whence the water for the dams is drawn; this water often is allowed to escape, having been polluted by flax, back again into the stream whence it was taken. The result in either case is the same. The rivulet conveys the poison to the river, or the river is poisoned from the leakage or overflow of the dams close to its banks. All through Eastern Ulster may be seen splendid rapid rivers once filled with salmon and trout, now without a fish of any sort from one year's end to the other. No doubt in one or two cases where the salmon fisheries are of great value, a number of bailiffs are employed who see that no leakage from dams or steeping in streams takes place. But in most places nothing of the sort is done, and the farmers steep flax how and where they like. The fact that flax is grown to a less extent than formerly does not help the fisheries, as flax water is so poisonous that a very small quantity destroys fish.

The sea-fishermen complain that fish avoid the bays or lochs, because of the poisonous filth poured into them by the rivers at certain seasons. There is a great and growing discontent among the coast population on this subject.

Ulster farmers are generally fond of horse-dealing in a small way. What is termed " feeding a horse " is a practice peculiar to the north of Ireland. A horse is shut up in a darkened stable, and is stuffed with everything he can eat, often getting spices and drugs to stimulate his appetite and improve his coat. He is sold at the summer fairs to English dealers, when the animal is generally as fat as a prize bullock. The more common practice is, for the average peasant farming thirty or forty acres, to keep one horse all the year round, and to buy another one during autumn. This young animal is half-worked and well-fed during the winter, ploughing in small fields of light land merely develops his muscles, and when the spring work is over he is usually sold at a profit. The farm is small, and the greater part is usually under grass, so that a pair of light half, or three-quarter bred horses can do all the necessary labour. Of late years many brood mares are kept, and farmers are anxious to breed good horses, but they are not encouraged in this or anything else.

The landlords are absentees and don't interest themselves in their estates, and the stallions sent by the State through the country are very second-rate animals.

Pigs in Ulster, instead of being driven or led to fairs, as in other parts of Ireland, are killed at home, and the dead pork is carted to the market, where it is bought for bacon-curing firms.

The semi-ownership of their land by the cultivators, which has been always more or less recognised by the landlord, constitutes Ulster landholders as a class peculiar to this part of the British Islands. They are somewhat independent, if not rude, in manner, and men holding farms of not more than sixty or seventy acres are often quite rich for men in their position. Peasants sometimes die worth a few thousand pounds, and five hundred pounds is often given as a marriage portion. Side by side with such men, even on the same estate, are others, head over ears in debt. In a state of society like this, where every one does as he likes with his land, subject to the payment of a yearly rent, much depends on individual character. The tenant has to do everything for himself just as though he were a settler or colonist, as in point of fact he is. The " office " of the agent is to the tenant much as a department of the State would be elsewhere. The rent is paid there, and aid of any kind is neither sought nor given. So far as

Ulster is, and always has been, concerned, the landlord or office confers no benefit on the community. This being so, the intelligent and thrifty man succeeds, whilst the idle and thriftless man fails. Land is for the most part easily worked and fertile in these settlements, and it is the custom for the people to work it "amongst themselves." This means that the farmer and his family all work in the fields, the women weed flax, gather potatoes, and bind up corn, as well as making butter, and attending to poultry. The result is that an industrious family, with a farm of sixty or seventy acres of fertile land at a fair rent, must make money. They hire no labour, save that of the cottar for a few days in seed or harvest-time. The farm supplies all necessaries unless dress and a few groceries, and the people are saving in their habits and care little for pleasure. The state of society in these districts is more Continental than British. And the Ulster peasant has little in common with the tenant farmer of other parts of the British Isles. I use the term peasant because it best describes these people; it is the term used abroad for men owning or partly owning their farms. And these Ulster men in most respects resemble the better class of French, Belgian, or German peasants. But it must be always remembered that these men are limited to certain districts, and that the greater part of Ulster is like the rest of Ireland.

Ulster differs also from other parts of Ireland in having mills and small manufactories scattered up and down over its north-eastern portion. This is one reason why a class of tenants who are bad tenants all over the rest of Ireland are the best possible class of holders in Ulster. These are men renting farms of from two or three to four or five acres. They have not land enough to live by, therefore they have to work either at a trade or in some oat, flax-scutching, or other mill. A horse is not needed for so small a holding, and when other employment is slack, it can be worked with a spade. Spade culture is well known to be the best, therefore the crops are good. Vegetables are grown which are good for the pig ; a little cow is also kept. The rent is trifling—three or four pounds a year—and this is nearly always punctually paid, not being difficult to make up. The family work during seed and harvest time, and the amount of crop being small, little time is spent at it, so that there is time for other jobs for farmers. I have had some experience of men of this class, and have always found them to be excellent tenants and good citizens. I know no stronger argument in favour of "three acres and a cow," than just to point to one of these men. Two things are needful, so that such a man as I have tried to describe, may be able to make a living. One is, that he must have at least fairly good land, and the other is that he must be able to get a certain amount of employment.

I have known of one or two instances of men who gave all their time to the spade culture of four or five acres, and who did well ; but they were very strong and industrious men, and their land was very good and easily worked. Unless near large towns where a market can be found for fruit or vegetables, the very small holder generally wants some employment outside that to be found on his little farm.

Ulster men are very litigious, much more so than the inhabitants of the rest of Ireland. A rich Ulster peasant always tries to make one of his sons a lawyer, and men of that calling abound in every town. There are constant petty lawsuits about everything for which an action at law can possibly be brought. I have known instances in which men have nearly beggared themselves by litigation about some trifle. Peasant wills, where a few pounds hoarded together, or a little " plenishing " or furniture, were in dispute, or quarrels about rights of way are the common grounds of action. There is very little crime of any kind. In such cases that occur, the friends of the accused spare neither cost nor trouble in their defence.

Ulster also differs from the rest of Ireland as to accent and dialect. The common north of Ireland accent is to be found over the greater part of the province, although some whole counties and parts of others are free from it. The dialects, which are for the most part old-fashioned Scotch, are to be found in a few districts in the north and east.

In many parts of this province the people talk with the usual Irish accent of the west and central portions of the Island. There are very few parts of Leinster in which the people are more Celtic in manner and appearance than some of the Ulster Irish. Excepting in Donegal, the Erse or Irish language is little spoken in Ulster, although half a century ago there were said, on good authority, to have been Irish-speaking people in the mountains of Eastern Ulster.

# CHAPTER IV.

BY resources here are meant, not the general resources
of Ireland, which have been treated of in many a
bulky volume, but simply the chief means the people
have of paying their rents and of buying necessaries.

It is a common idea that the pig of the south and
the flax of the north are the "great props and sup-
ports of Ireland." The stale old story of the "gentlemen who pay the rent" is still kept up for the benefit
of tourists by vendors of small pigs carved in bog
oak. Now, as a matter of fact, the pig plays but a
small part in Irish rural economy. Horned cattle are
the main resource of Ireland, and the cattle-dealer
and cattle-salesman are very important persons in
that country. Cattle are the great wealth of Ireland,
from the huge animal fattening on the fertile plains
of Meath to the dwarfed starveling running on the
barren mountains which rise from the Atlantic.
Horses and sheep come next in value, and a long way
behind comes the pig.

All these animals vary greatly in both size and
quality. There are some very large cattle and sheep
on the rich pastures, and some equally small and
stunted on the mountains and hilly places. The
same with horses; some of the best hunters to be

found anywhere are Irish horses, some of the most miserable screws are also to be found in Ireland. All these animals find buyers. To certain districts in England and Scotland none but good cattle are shipped. To other places few are sent save those of inferior or middling quality. All kinds of Irish horses are in demand, from the weight-carrying hunter to the smallest pony or hack. They have all an amount of staying powers and hardiness not to be found in English horses. The reason for this, per-haps, will be found in the fact that there is so little "cart blood" in Ireland.

In 1890, the numbers of cattle, sheep, and pigs were—

|  | | Cattle. | Sheep. | Pigs. |
|---|---|---|---|---|
| Leinster, | . | 1,059,810 | 1,391,196 | 373,392 |
| Connaught, | . | 676,260 | 1,320,573 | 252,703 |
| Munster, | . | 1,402,730 | 1,006,340 | 525,205 |
| Ulster, | . | 1,101,516 | 605,286 | 419,066 |
|  | | 4,240,316 | 4,323,395 | 1,570,366 |

There were also 584,872 horses.

It is not found possible to state exactly the values of these animals. Cattle and horses vary in price from day to day; sharp and sudden falls in prices taking place with, at certain times, equally rapid rises.

The ancient Irish cattle are nearly extinct, except in the southernmost part of the island, where they are called "Kerries." At one time, cattle of this variety, that is, black, red, or dun in colour, with long horns, were common to every part of Ireland. Many old people have told me that they remembered droves of the old, black, Irish breed of cattle where not one is now to be found. The same or nearly the same variety of cattle are common to all Celtic countries. In the Highlands of Scotland are found the West Highland and Kyloe breeds of cattle, both resembling the ancient Irish animals. In Wales are found a similar kind of black and dun-coloured cattle ; and lastly, in Brittany are found a breed of cattle closely resembling the foregoing British varieties.

In Ireland the original breed of cattle have been nearly altogether displaced by the introduction from time to time of successive strains of shorthorn blood. This latter element now largely prevails in most Irish cattle. Many persons well acquainted with the subject are in favour of retaining the ancient variety in the hilly and poorer districts.

Shorthorns are " too good " for such places, and the cross-bred animals are often found to be of a very worthless quality. They grow more quickly than do the old variety ; hence the people generally prefer them. Little attention has of late years been paid to the improvement of Irish stock, and its quality is nothing like as good as it was. Public attention has been so absorbed in politics that there seemed to be time for nothing else.

The largest Irish cattle are usually exported fat to Liverpool, where some are killed and salted for ship beef. Others find their way to the large towns of the North of England, where they meet with a ready sale. These are not the best quality of Irish cattle. They are the largest animals, but their flesh is often coarse. The finest quality of Irish cattle are shipped in a partly fat state—some to Aberdeen and parts of Scotland, where they are fattened on cake and turnips during the winter, and sent to London as "Scotch beef." Others find their way to the Leicestershire pastures, and many of what are called store cattle go to Norfolk and the eastern counties. Inferior and lean animals are sent to the Cumberland fells and to other parts of the north-west of England.

The comparative mildness and dampness of the Irish climate is found to be favourable for raising stock. It is quite a mistake to suppose that cattle are chiefly to be found in the grazing districts. As may be seen from the foregoing table, there are more horned cattle in Ulster than in either Leinster or Connaught, although the chief grazing tracts are in these two latter provinces. The fact is that cattle can be raised better by small tillage farmers than by graziers. That is when the farmer is a good agriculturist, and grows plenty of turnips. This most good Ulster farmers do. The consequence is that their cattle are well wintered, and are much better cared for than those of the grazier, who is often a mere jobber or land-grabber, and whose cattle run over bare pastures during the winter, and get at most a little coarse hay.

Ireland is, for the most part, a pastoral country. There is a greater proportion of land under crop in Ulster than in any of the other three provinces. Yet even in Ulster little more than a fourth part of its whole extent is under tillage in any one year. In 1890, out of 5,322,321 acres, the extent of Ulster, 1,741,125 acres were under crop, including hay on permanent pastures, or meadows. Out of 4,838,510 acres in Leinster, 1,331,601 were under crop. From this it will be seen that the proportion of grass to tillage differs little in either of these provinces. In the remaining provinces the proportion of grass is yet greater.

Compared with pigs, butter, flax, and other Irish products, cattle vary greatly in price. In some years those who buy cattle to graze or fatten on the summer pastures make money easily and without trouble. In other years they lose heavily, rent of the grazing, part of the cost of the stock, and last, not least, interest on the capital employed, all go. This latter item is often a very serious one, as the capital wherewith to stock large grass farms is often borrowed from banks at high interest.

As pork and corn are in America, pig-iron in Glasgow, and cotton in Liverpool, so are cattle in Ireland. They are the staple trade of the country, whose pastures are matchless. They are also unhappily little better than pawns on a chessboard, as there is too much jobbing on borrowed money in the cattle trade. Jobbers or dealers in cattle are of different sorts. A peasant may deal in two or three calves at a time, or a big dealer may ship two or three hundred large beasts on a steamer at a time. There are also cattle salesmen, chiefly in Dublin, to whom large quantities of cattle are consigned for sale from distant parts of the country. Sometimes the market is glutted, and many persons having grazing land near Dublin make a trade of buying stock in a "slack market and selling in a brisk one."

The original owner of the stock living at a great distance must let his stock go for what it will fetch. But the man who has his farm near Dublin can drive his stock home, if they do not make a price that pleases him, and try his chance on another day.

Many, if not most people in Ireland, depend more or less on cattle for a livelihood. Were it not for this trade, few of the many cross channel steamers now trading between England and Ireland could be kept up, save at a heavy loss. The employment given to drovers, quay porters, and others is a very important matter in a country like Ireland. Almost all the rural population, whether peasant, cow-jobber, or shopkeeper, are deeply moved by the ups and downs in the price of cattle. "What sort of crops have they across the channel?" is one of the first questions asked of anyone who has lately "crossed." Much depends on these crops; if they are good, cattle, to be fattened or finished on Norfolk or Aberdeen turnips and cake, will be in demand. Prices of stock will be high, and everyone have some money. If English crops are bad, cattle will be in little demand, prices will fall, and everyone in rural Ireland will suffer more or less thereby.

Of the native Irish sheep little is known. The kinds now most to be seen in Ireland are Leicesters, Shropshire downs, horned blackface Scotch, and a variety called the "Roscommon." This is a very large sheep, and is said to be descended from the native sheep crossed with Leicester. As may be seen from the table, most Irish sheep are in the province of Connaught, the dry limestone pastures of this province being found particularly suited to these animals.

The Irish horse is a very well-known animal, and usually bears a good character. Nevertheless, his history is a somewhat difficult and obscure one. The question has been asked, was there an original variety of this animal peculiar to Ireland ? in other words, was there such a thing as the "old Irish horse?" Many good authorities are of opinion that there was such an animal, and profess to be able to discover many of his points in the horses now to be found in Ireland. This old blood is chiefly to be found in hunters. The jumping powers of the Irish hunter are well known. He jumps, in the true sense of the word, that is, like a deer ; he does not "fly his fences" as many very highly-bred horses do. There are yet to be found in the west of Ireland horses, not lengthy or very fast gallopers, but wonderfully good jumpers of walls. They are able usually to clear a stone wall five feet high. It is difficult to discover the descent of these animals. Horses have been so crossed and recrossed that the pedigree becomes lost in a maze. One thing is certain, that from some source the Irish hunter inherits a capacity and style of jumping that is unrivalled.

As in Wales and Scotland, there are many good ponies in Ireland.[1] The best of these are to be found either in Antrim or Connemara. With the best intentions on the part of certain landowners, the ponies have been greatly spoiled by the introduction of Suffolk Punches among them. The Suffolk Punch

[1] See appendix G.

may be all very well in his way, but crossed with mountain pony he becomes a failure. Such an animal is neither draught horse nor pony, and has often all the bad qualities of both. The black or dun-coloured northern ponies are excellent when they can be obtained of pure blood. They have all the good qualities of the Shetland pony, but are of much greater size, being often over fourteen hands high. There is little doubt but that the pony is the original British horse, varying in size in different parts of these islands. The earlier English horses seem to have been coarse draught animals chiefly from Flanders. Arabian and Barb blood is of comparatively recent introduction, and the English thoroughbred is quite a modern class of animal. It is possible that the old Irish horse may be descended from a cross of pony and some of the earlier thoroughbreds brought into Ireland two centuries ago. This is merely a conjecture, but I have heard good authorities in Yorkshire remark that some of the best hunters were often the offspring of pony mares. The only really Irish horses are the true Irish hunters, when they can be found, and the pony. Most horses now to be found in Ireland are descended from recently imported thoroughbred and cart horses. Neither of these latter are of the highest quality. They are second if not third-rate animals for the greater part; their progeny form good, useful horses, suitable for troopers or hacks, and pay the breeder fairly well. Large droves of such horses are bought at the great fairs every year by Belgian, French, German, and English buyers. They are afterwards used for troop

horses or harness horses of moderate price. Good
hunters are rather scarce and command high prices.
Middling hunters are common enough. It is a growing practice to breed a horse half, or quarter, cart,
such as Clydesdale, and the rest thoroughbred. The
thoroughbred strain is not the highest, and horses
bred in this way are but of indifferent quality.
They look well, often better, than animals far their
superiors, and, therefore, sell at good prices to people
who do not really understand horses. If the Irish
horse is to be improved, or even if the character of
the good hunters is to be kept up, either the State
or private individuals should import thoroughbred
horses of the highest breeding, and of great size and
bone. It is a matter of the greatest moment to
Ireland that the character of her horses should be
kept up; they are among the few things for which she
gets credit.

From the great extent of level grass land, and
bottoms or " callows," as they are called in Ireland, it is
a country peculiarly well suited for breeding horses,
and even in agricultural parts of the country farmers
often raise a very useful class of animals. But here
again politics and a state of unrest interfere, and
these noble animals do not meet with that attention
and kindness which is their due. If a young horse is
to develop into anything valuable, he must be well
cared for in every respect, and this is a fact that
many persons in Ireland have yet to learn.

One animal now remains to be described, and that
is the pig. Of the four species which form the great
wealth of the Irish people, this is the least important.

At one time the ancient Irish pig was well known, and even yet there are places where he may be seen. He was, or is, plainly the lineal descendant of a wild species, and his blood seemed to be for the most part pure and unmixed. He had long legs, a very high arched back, flat sides, and a long snout. His bristles were of great length, and his disposition was of a fierce nature. To one unused to the appearance of such an animal he seemed partly repulsive and partly grotesque. From the length of his legs and general lightness of his build, he must have possessed great speed, and in a wild state should afford good sport. He is now nearly extinct, and the modern Irish pig is usually a cross of the common English varieties with the native race. Some of these are black, others are white, and they are considered to make good bacon.

In the south of Ireland, pigs are driven to fair or market and bought by bacon-curing firms in the southern towns, and some are shipped alive, chiefly from Waterford, to England. In northern Ireland, pigs are killed at home, as already stated, and are bought by bacon-curers in the Ulster towns. They are sold by weight, so much per hundred. Pigs are not generally considered to pay when all their food has to be bought. They are only supposed to be profitable for land-holders, who have refuse, potatoes, milk, and meal of their own. There are no doubt many cases of small holders in the south of Ireland where the pig pays the rent. But to say that he generally, or to any great extent does so, is absurd.

There is a great quantity of butter made in Ireland, much of which is used at home. There have been many complaints as to the way in which Irish butter has been packed for exportation, also as to the manner in which it has been made. Of late years, educational dairies have been established, and the quality of the butter much improved. This has been done by private individuals much to their credit. What effect these institutions may yet have it is now impossible to state, but for so far they are found to be fairly successful.

The process of steeping and scutching flax has been already mentioned. Having been made ready, it is sold in the markets to flax-buyers. When all expenses are paid it yields little profit to the grower, and forms a comparatively small item in the list of peasant resources. It must be borne in mind that out of the gross sum yielded by the sale of flax must be taken the cost of labour and preparing. This is very great, and it is a common thing for a farmer to be actually out of pocket by his flax.

In the eastern and north-eastern parts of Ireland, corn is grown to some extent. The climate of these parts of the country is comparatively dry, and fairly good samples of grain can be grown. In the west and south-west of Ireland a little oats is grown, but the quality is bad as a rule ; the best oats being grown in the north of Ireland. Wheat and barley are grown in the eastern districts ; the former is generally too damp for grinding by itself, but when mixed with foreign grain it can be ground. Much of it is used in the manufacture of starch, being too damp for any other purpose. Barley always finds a ready sale at the Dublin breweries, always provided that it has not been too much spoiled by wet. As Dublin breweries make porter for the most part, there is not the same necessity that barley should have a bright colour as there is in England.

Rye is grown to some extent in boggy districts, the peat soil being well suited for its growth. The grain is used for making whisky, and the straw for thatch. Rye straw thatch is said to last for many years, and a coating of it is supposed to outlast several coatings of either wheat or oat straw. There may be such a thing as rye-bread in Ireland, but if there is I never heard of it. Unlike the Continental peasantry, the Irish rural population have no idea of eating black bread.

Beetroots and mangel-wurzel both grow well in Ireland, but comparatively small spaces are sown with either. Irish beetroot contains little saccharine matter as compared with that grown on the Continent. Want of sun is said to be the cause.

Potatoes are not grown to as great an extent as is commonly supposed. In the south and west they form the chief food of the people, but they are not grown to any great extent for sale or export. In the eastern parts of Ireland potatoes are grown to a larger extent, and are sold in Dublin and other towns and cities. Some are also exported to England. The soil along many parts of the eastern shore of Ireland is light, and therefore well suited for potatoes, which are generally sound and free from disease. In no part of Ireland that I have seen are potatoes so extensively grown as in parts of Lincolnshire and Scotland, where they form a considerable item among the exports from those parts of Great Britain.

There is very little fruit grown in Ireland.  In no
part of the British Isles are orchards less common,
and gardens in the rural districts are almost unknown.
The Irish people generally display no taste for the culture of either fruit or flowers.  Where there have been
orchards they have in many places been either grubbed
up or allowed to run wild.  I knew of an instance in
the north of Ireland where a man grubbed up a nice-
looking little orchard.  His defence for doing so was
that there were so few fruit trees anywhere for miles
round that boys came from great distances to rob his
apple-trees.  He also said that the orchard ground
would pay much better under crop.

In some parts of Ireland there are such things as
orchards which receive a certain amount of care.  But
these localities are few and very limited in extent.

In the neighbourhood of Dublin cabbages are largely
grown, and there are great " cabbage gardens," as they
are called.  These are fields, often several acres in extent, wholly devoted to the growing of different kinds
of cabbages.  There seems to be a supply of one sort
or another nearly all the year round, and from the
great depth and fertility of the soil the cabbages are
of good quality.  These cabbage fields afford employment to a great number of persons, as many of them
are cultivated with the spade.  Women are also employed for weeding and other work.  Onions and
other vegetables are also cultivated, but not to any
great extent.  The cabbages find a ready market in
Dublin and its suburbs, and great quantities of greens
are exported to Liverpool and Glasgow, especially to
the latter city.  They are packed in large open

"crates" made of wooden rails, about two inches in diameter. This cabbage trade is a larger one than people think, and might be greatly extended. The neighbourhood of Dublin is very well suited for market gardening, being on the western and northern sides, level, fertile, and well sheltered. Its nearness to the sea also prevents frosts having the same effects as in more inland localities. Fruit and vegetables of different kinds could also be grown here to a much greater extent than at present.

The foregoing are the chief resources of rural Ireland. How these resources are capable of development is a question somewhat difficult to answer. Agriculture seems to be unsuited to the greater part of the island. The climate is too damp, and prices are too low for grain to be successfully cultivated. Farmers seem to have discovered this fact already, for the quantity of land under grain crops gets less every year. The improvement of the existing breeds of cattle and horses, and the extension of market gardening in the neighbourhoods of the chief seaports, would seem to be the best means of further developing Irish resources. Drainage and the reclamation of land in central Ireland, and in some places along the coast, would also confer a great benefit on the country.

# CHAPTER V.

THE powers of local bodies and authorities in Ireland are usually very limited. The country is practically ruled from Dublin in nearly every respect, local governing authorities being all controlled from thence. These local authorities are, Boards of Poor Law Guardians and Grand Juries in the rural districts, and Corporations and Town Commissioners in cities and towns.

Boards of Guardians, elected and ex-officio, correspond with the same kind of authorities in England; but in Ireland they are ruled to a great extent by a central Poor Law Board in Dublin. The Irish Poor Law system is now something less than half a century old, and has been from the first thoroughly unpopular. The reason perhaps is, that it is modelled to some extent on the English system, and that what works well in England may not suit Ireland. It is a generally acknowledged fact that the Irish people for the most part are unlike the English. Irish ideas on most matters are Continental rather than British, and the mass of the Irish rural population have more in common with France than with England.

Public relief is looked on by the English poor as a right to which they are entitled, and the period of change from old to new is centuries of age. In Ireland the system is new and has been introduced contrary to the wishes of the people, whose whole sentiment and feelings are in favour of almsgiving. To accept the relief offered by the workhouse is looked on as something disgraceful, although no shame is felt in accepting private charity, or even in begging. Almsgiving is in most parts of Ireland thought to be just as needful as though no rates were paid for poor relief, so that the peasant is doubly taxed. He pays poor rates and yet gives alms to perhaps as great an extent as the Continental peasant who is not rated in the same way.

One great reason for the unpopularity of the Irish Poor Law system is the fact that outdoor relief is seldom or never allowed. Now in this respect the English system is much more liberal. There, outdoor relief, such as it is, is more common than in Ireland. It seems very cruel to force decent poor people into the " house," their horror and hatred of which cannot be described. And the length of time that has passed since the introduction of the Poor Law system has done nothing to lessen this feeling. Poor folk will drag on a miserable existence for months on cold potatoes or scraps given by their neighbours, nor until they are ejected from their wretched hovels will they seek the shelter of the "house." This system is in every way useless, as well as causing needless suffering and bitter discontent. Many people will say that outdoor relief degrades and pauperises; the "house" does so far more. Take an instance from real life. A decent family is in dire need from accident, illness,

or unforeseen misfortunes of some sort. Outdoor
relief is as a matter of course refused. These unhappy people, often affectionate, religious, and well-
behaved, are after a short struggle obliged to enter
the workhouse. Here husband, wife, and children are
separated from one another, and the latter, generally
innocent little rustics, are ruined perhaps for life by
contact with workhouse children. Here then are
human lives blighted for ever, for no good reason
that anyone can see. This is no fancy description,
such cases are but too well known. By giving outdoor relief for a few months, the period of distress
might have been tided over, the home saved, and the
children preserved from moral destruction.

In England rates are levied over the whole Union,
in Ireland they are " struck " or levied for each Poor
Law electoral division ; as already stated, the parish
has been disused for civil purposes. In England the
tenant pays all the poor rates, in Ireland the landlord
pays a half, so that in this respect the Irish tenant is
much better off. In fairly good districts in Ireland
poors rates are lower than in England. In parts of
Ulster they often do not exceed ninepence or tenpence
in the pound. From the great dislike of the workhouse, there are comparatively few paupers in Irish
Unions. From an electoral division in Ulster, which
was several miles across either way, there was at one
time but a single pauper in the workhouse. It was
found on looking at the rateable value of the division,
that a rate of less than a farthing in the pound, would
have given a cottage rent free and fifteen shillings a
week to this pauper. The average number of paupers

for a term of years from this district ranged from nil to two or three.

Irish workhouses appear to be much larger than those in the rural parts of England. They are gloomy, ugly buildings, and all are built in the same style. They are generally to be found in the out-skirts of a small country village or town.

There is a medical officer for each division; he is appointed by the Board of Guardians, and is but poorly paid. He has a private practice as well, but this is not worth much for different reasons. Doctors complain that persons well able to pay get tickets for gratuitous medical advice.[1] These tickets are given by Guardians to those who are in need of medical advice and are unable to pay for it.

The workhouse is just as unpopular with the farmers and ratepayers generally as with the poor. It is thought by many people that if there were no workhouses, the poor could be much more cheaply kept under a system of outdoor relief. The work-house officials are said to be costly, and not fully employed, the house being often not half full. Certainly, if calculations are made as to the cost of the number of paupers, and the salary of the medical officer, including all allowances for sundry small duties which he performs, it will be found that less than half the present rates levied will pay the doctor and keep the pauper. This may not be the case everywhere, but it is so in very many instances.

The present workhouse system may be right or wrong, for anything I know; of one thing I am cer-

---

[1] See correspondence in *Irish Times*, January 1892.

tain, and that is, that the system is generally unpopular.

Highways and the making of new roads and county works generally are ruled in this way. First what are called presentments are made—these are estimates by contractors and others for doing certain work. These works include keeping the highways in repair, and laying down thereon a certain number of broken stones, making new roads, cutting down hills on roads already made, or filling up hollows on the same, building bridges, making culverts and drains, also footpaths, and other things of the same kind. Roads are let in certain lengths to contractors to keep in order, and each bridge, cutting, culvert, footpath, or drain, is separately tendered for. All these tenders, from that for keeping a mile or two of a bye-road in order, to a tender for a bridge or hill cutting, are brought before the presentment sessions. These are held twice yearly, in certain villages or towns, situated in certain baronies. As already stated, the barony is the unit for county rating. Each barony has its own presentment sessions, at which the magistrates of that barony sit, together with what are called associated cess-payers. These are a chosen few of the largest ratepayers, appointed by the grand jury. The contracts are considered by this joint board; some are passed and others are thrown out. It is usual to pass the contracts for repairing the roads as a matter of course. The larger jobs are often fiercely contested, some of the board being in favour of economy, others of reckless expenditure. The estimates having passed, the presentment sessions are next considered by the grand jury, who may further alter them, and reject contracts passed at the sessions. Works of great public necessity are often blocked by this body for reasons best known to itself. This system is very unpopular with the bulk of the ratepayers, but with grand jurors it is popular enough. The great objections commonly made are, first, that the grand jury are not a popularly elected body, being chosen by the high sheriff. Next, that the greater number of votes at the presentment sessions are those of the associated cess-payers, who are chosen by the grand jury, the number of these cess-payers being generally in excess of that of the magistrates.[1] The result of this system is that all county business is practically ruled by the grand jury. It is the almost universal opinion of the great body of ratepayers that this rule is unsatisfactory. The general complaint is that too much rates are paid, and that too little work is done for the money. In a matter of this sort it is difficult to apportion the blame. The fault may lie with the grand jury system, or with the system of contracting, or with the surveyors of these public works, who may not look after the contractors as they ought. Two things are certain: one is that in the east and north-east of Ireland, which are the most civilised parts, the rates are as high, and the roads are kept in a worse manner than is the case in England. Any person can easily satisfy himself on these points. Wide main roads may be seen full of hollows or holes, the mud which has been scraped off from time to time lying dried in banks on either side. Between

[1] See appendix H,

the ruts and hollows, and the heaps and banks of dried mud, it must be a service of danger to drive along these roads on dark nights. Why the mud should not be carted away seems incomprehensible. It is generally thought by farmers that road scrapings, especially when roads pass through fertile districts as these do, are valuable for topdressing land. Yet here are the scrapings of years past lying along the roadside in heaps and ridges, to the great danger of the public. If the Irish farmers are too indifferent to take away this road stuff, it could be used to fill up hollows, or even be thrown into the sea which is not far off. Not very far from these roads may be seen places banked out from the sea, where stuff of the kind would be most useful to fill up the low-lying spaces. Everywhere I have been through eastern Ireland the roads are bad, particularly where there is much traffic. Some exceptions may be found on granitic formations, where the roads are naturally good.

Though the landlord in Ireland pays half the poor rates, the tenant, in most cases, pays all the county cess or highway rates. This latter is usually heavy, for though poor rates, as a rule, are lighter than in England, this is by no means the case with highway rates. Instances could be proved where highway rates in some of the midland parts of England were actually lower than in some rural parts of Ulster. In the former cases, though there was a much greater traffic on the roads, they were better kept and at a lesser cost. Excepting in rare instances on certain geological formations, such as sandstone or granite, Irish roads are rough and bad,

The composition of the grand jury varies greatly in different parts of Ireland. Where the landowners are absentees, their places are supplied by their agents, these men being supposed to be the deputies or representatives of their employers. This is an idea quite peculiar to Ireland, and accounts to a great extent for the arrogance of the Irish agent. The great landowners being almost always absentees, it follows that the greatest amount of property is represented on the grand jury by land-agents. Next to the agents come landowners of different sorts, many of them being very small proprietors. Some of these are "new men" who live in towns or their suburbs, others live in the country districts. None of these men occupy much land, as, except in a few counties, it is not the fashion for landlords to farm. Some of the grand jurors pay but a small proportion of the rates themselves; others are found who pay no highway rates in the county in which their property is situated. Now, as the tenant as a rule pays all the highway rates, and the landlord or agent, as a rule, pays little or none, it follows that grand jurors have not much interest in looking after county works and businesses. This is the tenant's view of the matter. He also strongly objects to the associated cess-payer as being the nominee of the grand jury. Though many associated cess-payers may be found who are strongly in favour of the reform of county government.

There is a surveyor for each county, who has several assistants under him. These men may often be seen driving about on hired cars, and seem to be always going somewhere. They are allowed (so I have been told) to do work privately on their own account. There is no reason to suppose that this interferes much with the performance of their public duties. It has only been said of the assistants, and the quantity of private work which they could obtain in Ireland must be very little.

It would be difficult to discover who is to blame. Perhaps no person is in fault, and the whole system is wrong. Be this as it may, the three facts stand forth—*i.e.*, bad roads, high rates, and public discontent. With farmers and others, who use these roads, and must see how they are cared for, the present system of management is very unpopular.

These two systems—*i.e.*, poor relief, and county roads and works, are the only kinds of local government in rural Ireland. Under the first system, the public are allowed to elect the greater number of the Guardians. In the latter system, the public have practically no voice. As county cess is the largest rate paid in the country districts of Ireland, it is but reasonable that, on this ground only, the public should claim a share in the local government of the county. Although people are all but unanimous in condemning the present system, they are by no means so as to the form of local government to be put in its place. The total abolition of the fiscal authority of the grand jury, which means practically effacing that body, is the chief thing on which most persons are agreed. They may also be said to be agreed on the principle of rates being levied by elected representatives of the people.

A local police force of a civil nature, and the control thereof by the local authority, is also called for by the majority of the rural public. It is thought by many that this should form a part of any scheme of local government. In order to understand fully this idea on the part of the rustic population, it will be needful to give a brief account of the present Irish police force. The rural police or constabulary are in some respects a military force; they have rifles and bayonets, swords and pistols. They are also drilled to a certain extent, though they cannot be said to manœuvre very well. They are under the rule of inspectors, some of whom are promoted from the force, others admitted by examination. These in·spectors receive their orders from Dublin Castle and are altogether independent of the local authorities. The men, instead of being quartered singly or in twos or threes, like the English constabulary, are quartered in sixes or greater numbers in barracks, situated in villages for the most part. A patrol of two policemen leaves each village in the evening and walks along a highroad, where it meets another patrol from the nearest barracks in that direction. Having met, each patrol then returns to its own barracks. It is a common idea that Ireland is full of crime and disturbance, and needs a powerful and well-armed police force in every part. This is quite a false notion. With the exception of some half-dozen counties out of thirty-two, and a few districts in others where there have been special causes for trouble, Ireland is a quiet country. This will be best understood from the following figures. From January 1st to December

31st, 1890, but *fifty-one* outrages and crimes were
reported in the province of Ulster; out of these there
were *ten* convictions. In Leinster during the same
year, were *fifty-six* crimes with *four* convictions.
In Munster were *two hundred and ninety* crimes
with *fifteen* convictions. In Connaught, there were
one hundred and twenty-two crimes and six convictions. From these figures it will appear that Leinster
and Ulster are nearly free from crime, and that the
chief amount is found in Munster and Connaught.
It also appears from the returns of offences that 273
out of 290 were committed or reported in four Munster counties, leaving but 24 or an average of 12 for
the remaining two, and that 72 out of 122 crimes
were reported in one county of Connaught, leaving
but 50 crimes or an average of 12¼ for each of the
other four counties. We thus find that there are but
five counties in Ireland in which any serious quantity
of crime is to be found. If the history and average
returns of criminal offences for the last quarter of a
century are studied, it will be found that the disturbed
or criminal area in Ireland has always been a small
one.

Returns of crimes for different years vary somewhat. In times of great excitement or great want,
more crime is committed than in better or more restful
times. Besides this the area of discontent and crime
shifts its ground now and then, or there may be
special causes for riot and outrage in certain districts.
But on the whole it will be found that the disturbed
area has been very much in the same place for many
years past. Any person well acquainted with Ireland

is familiar with those counties known respectively as quiet and disorderly.

These offences include murder, manslaughter, firing at the person, attempted murder, assaults of different kinds, maiming or cutting, arson, housebreaking, burglary, robbery, taking forcible possession, cattle-stealing, sheep-stealing, injuries to cattle, demanding arms, riots, unlawful oaths, intimidation, threatening letters and notices by intimidation or otherwise, breach of pound, attacks on houses, resistance to legal processes, injuries to property, firing into dwellings, injuries to places of worship, or to highways or to telegraph wires, perjury, injury to railways. This list includes, as may be seen, every sort of crime and offence, unless those of a trivial nature.[1]

It will be seen from these figures that the number of convictions is very small compared with the number of crimes and outrages reported. Some persons might draw the conclusions from this, either that the Irish police force was very inefficient or incapable, or that the reports of crimes were untrue, and that, therefore, Ireland was a strangely peaceful country.

It has seemed to many people in Ireland that, however well the present force may be suited for maintaining order in the disturbed parts of the country, it is quite unsuited to the greater part of Ireland. So many Irishmen now go backwards and forwards between their own country and England that the idea has gained ground that Ireland should have the same rights and privileges as her sister. When Irishmen

---

[1] Returns of Agrarian crime for 1890. Dublin: Alex. Thom Why called " agrarian " it would be hard to say.

find in England an elected county council, and a few
quiet "bobbies" controlled by local authorities, they
naturally think that they also should have the same;
particularly when they find these things in English
counties not nearly so peaceful as many in Ireland.[1]
It is also thought that a civil force quartered singly,
or in small numbers, as in England, would be much
more effective for the detection of ordinary crime
than the present force.

A complete scheme of local government should include, according to the ideas of most people on the
subject, the control of all local affairs. These are
usually considered to be, poor relief, roads, and other
local works and improvements, and the maintenance
of order or police. A system such as this is now to
be found in English towns and counties, and there
seems to be no reason why it should not be extended
to such Irish counties as can show a peaceful record
for a certain number of years. In the few counties
which have a bad record, local government as to roads
and public works might be at once granted, and the
control of the police withheld for some years.

Vestries, so far as public works are concerned, are,
and have always been, unknown in Ireland. Nor
could parish councils be very well set up in Ireland.
The parish is not a division for civil purposes now,
and villages are too far apart, and the electoral

---

[1] It is hardly necessary to mention the trades union outrages,
strike riots, poaching affrays, and other crimes which have dis-
graced the north counties of England for many years. Though
police in English counties are not controlled by the county
councils, they are locally controlled.

divisions too large for the latter to be made areas for local administration. It would be difficult to set up in rural Ireland smaller bodies than county councils. The people, being unused to having anything like vestries or parish councils, are very unlikely to call for anything of the sort. Councils for each barony might possibly be demanded, but as many baronies are as large as small counties, barony councils would amount to much the same thing as county councils.

Many Irish rural ratepayers are very intelligent, and quite capable of deciding on the best methods of road management. They have to use the roads as well as to pay for them, and are very unlikely to choose representatives who are not both honest and capable. Men of this sort are much more common in Ireland than is generally supposed, and there is no good reason for thinking that elected bodies throughout rural Ireland would be less competent than elsewhere. Why elected bodies such as Town Commissioners and Poor Law Guardians should manage important affairs, and people in the rural districts not be allowed to manage their roads, it is not easy to understand. And why a minority should fear a county council more than a Board of Guardians or Town Commissioners, is yet more difficult to comprehend. Yet such fears are expressed, and measures called for to protect minorities, in the event of county elected bodies being established in Ireland.

# CHAPTER VI.

## IRISH ESTATES AND THEIR INHABITANTS.

IRISH estates vary nearly, if not as much, as the appearance of the country itself. The chief landowners are absentee noblemen, men in business, chiefly lawyers and distillers, London companies, and lastly (a long way), those of the old Irish gentry who have escaped the effects of the great famine. Any reader of modern history must know of the great change that took place in the ownership of land in Ireland after the famine. It is not generally realised, though, how great an epoch it formed in the history of Ireland during the present century. Though more than a generation has passed since its closing years, the fearful memories of the famine yet rankle in the minds of the Irish race all over the world. The changes in the social life of Ireland which it wrought were great and many, but none greater than the wholesale revolution brought about as to the proprietorship of the soil. Great estates belonging to historic families were brought to the hammer and sold in lots to speculators in land, often yielding as much as seven and eight per cent. on the purchase money. Estate after estate was sold in the "encumbered estates' court" for almost what they would fetch. Old family mansions passed into the hands of cattle-dealers. Speculators and jobbers in land of all sorts bought in every direction. At first land was sold for very low prices, as times got better the demand improved, until of late years the "encumbered estates' court" became the "landed estates' court." This is practically a kind of mart in which the titles of estates are first enquired into, and, if these are found to be good, the lands are sold. They are not knocked down at the present day for anything they will bring; there is usually a reserve price under which the lands may not be sold. The title, having passed through the landed estates' court, is always considered to be good and safe. It is called a "landed estates' court title" and is supposed to be indefeasible.

The great change in the ownership of land took place during the years immediately following the famine. Afterwards the sales became much less in number, although down to the present time many estates change hands yearly.

Wonderful things were prophesied as to the "new owners." "The old thriftless, reckless, sporting squirearchy were replaced by new men, who had capital, intelligence, and all sorts of good qualities." Articles appeared in the newspapers as to the change for the better about to take place, the improvements to be made by these intelligent capitalists, and so on. However, recent history has falsified all these roseate forecasts. Instead of spending money on their estates, the new owners extracted much more out of them than their former proprietors had ever done. In old times rents had been paid frequently by small services rendered, now they had to be paid in hard cash. Everything was looked sharply into, and where land was found to have good grazing qualities, the tenants were evicted without getting a penny of compensation, and their farms were thrown into large grazing tracts. Everything was done on " business principles," and the new landlords exercised to the full all their legal powers. Nor were many of the older landowners slow to follow the example thus set them. The result was hostility between landowners and their tenants greater than had ever existed before, and men, forced to emigrate, left their country with hatred in their minds. It is needless to remark that this feeling has been handed down and been the cause of endless troubles in recent years.

Those landowners who survived the affects of the famine were either great landlords, many of whom had other property in England, or men having property in Ireland which was little affected by the famine. The latter were chiefly owners of land in the good grazing districts or in the bettermost parts of Ulster. The proportion of new owners varies greatly in different counties. Few of them own properties of any great extent. If the lists of landowners in Ireland are carefully studied it will be found that the large estates chiefly belong either to noblemen, who are for the most part absentees, or to the London companies in Ulster. But though new owners have each of them but small properties, yet in the aggregate a great extent of country is in their hands.

The great landowners are generally of ancient Irish, Norman Irish, or seventeenth century English or

Scotch descent. Some of these estates are very large, one being over one hundred and sixty thousand acres in extent, and there are several others of over one hundred thousand acres. [1]

Unless the very few great landowners of ancient Irish stock, nearly all these great landlords trace their titles from the forfeitures of the lands of the Irish chiefs. [2] This is a matter of history, and any person who wishes to pursue the subject further has but to study the history of Ireland from the reign of Henry II.

It would be difficult to find one of these great estates which might be looked on as a type of all. They are far apart, some in the extreme north and others in the south of Ireland, districts in which manners and customs differ widely. Nevertheless, there are some respects in which all agree. To begin with these. In the first place, there are small poor holdings more or less on all these great territorial estates. In the next place they are managed, or perhaps it would be more correct to state, ruled by a resident agent.

The small holder of parts of Ulster has been already

---

[1] Lord Donegall's estate is 162,961 acres.
   „   Conyngham's   „   156,973  „
   „   Lansdown's   „   121,349  „
   „   Kenmare's   „   118,606  „
and many others of from ninety to over one hundred thousand acres.

[2] Lord O'Niell and Lord Antrim among the great landowners, and the O'Conor Don and the O'Grady among the smaller landlords, may be mentioned as examples of men holding old estates which have not been escheated.

described, but something remains to be written about the small holder in other parts of Ireland. There is the small farmer, so-called, of the extreme west, who is unable to support himself on his holding and is obliged to go to England every year as a harvest-man. There are also in every poor and mountainous district in Ireland, Ulster included, a class of small holders, whose condition is little better than that of the "Connaught man." In addition to these there are some small holdings in comparatively good parts of Ireland. Now, it may be asked, why there are so many small farmers in Ireland, and why they should, for the most part, be crowded on to the worst parts of the island?

The history of small holders in Ireland is to a great extent political. At the close of the reign of James II., in contemporary accounts and journals, mention is made of vast, thinly-peopled, pastoral tracts being in places in which, in the present century, swarms of peasant holdings were to be found. How did this state of things come to pass? So far as can now be discovered, in two ways. First, by subdivision in order to multiply votes. Next, by letting large tracts of land to middlemen who sub-let at a profit. The first cause was the chief one. During the palmy days of the old Irish Parliament, election contests were fiercely fought. The tenants at that time always voted with their landlords, so that the man who commanded most votes was he who had the greatest number of tenants. The large owners led the way in cutting up their estates, the smaller owners followed in their wake. After the Union, the same kind of thing went on, potatoes were good and free from disease, emigration was almost unknown, and the population rapidly rose in numbers. On the abolition of the "forty shilling" freehold franchise, landlords ceased to encourage subdivision, especially as they had lost their political influence over the greater part of Ireland. However, the middleman still throve, and it suited him to carry on the old policy. How men in their senses could have wilfully destroyed their property by the twofold policy of subdivision and letting to middlemen it is difficult to imagine. And why the State allowed them to do so is yet harder to conceive. However, the State and the landlords and, yet more, the unhappy people, have suffered and are still suffering from the effects of this suicidal policy. The story of the Irish famine need not be gone into here. Enough to say that deaths and emigration soon thinned the population, which has fallen from some eight millions in 1841 to some five millions in 1871.

After the famine, the State and the new owners had a good opportunity of remedying matters, but the time was allowed to go by, and the chance was lost for ever. Middlemen had disappeared, the famine had extinguished them. The population was greatly lessened from the same cause, and quantities of land were in hand. Everything favoured a policy of moving people from poor districts and settling them in better localities, allotting the mountainous and poor districts into good-sized holdings, and strictly prohibiting subdivision, at the same time dividing the fertile plains into small farms on which people could make a comfortable living; in short, a policy of re-modelling and settling on a sound basis the whole Irish land system. Instead of doing this, a wholly different method was adopted. The State did nothing, save sell encumbered estates. The landlords, old and new, ejected people from land suitable for grazing, and allowed them to swarm and multiply in barren districts. For nearly a quarter of a century this policy was followed without let or hindrance. Murders and agrarian crime multiplied at a fearful rate. Nothing could be worse than the record of crime in certain districts. In old times riots and disturbances had been common, but the terrorism and assassinations of these modern times were nearly unknown. Nor, indeed, could they be wondered at. Wholesale clearances of the remaining population were made over wide tracts, the people getting no compensation for the loss of their homes. Large grazing districts now almost uninhabited may be seen which, at one time, supported thousands of people. Yet almost adjoining, are sterile mountains swarming with people in a state of want. It was considered that where the land was " no good," as much could be made by letting small tenants have it as in any other way. The result is that, though the population is less, and there are more large farms now than before the famine, yet the condition of the average small holder is no better, parts of Ulster always excepted. The constant famines on a small scale in the extreme south, west, and north-west of Ireland are so many proofs of this statement    Nor is distress confined to these districts. Some years ago a clergyman in a mountainous part of one of the best Ulster counties wrote to the local newspapers appealing for aid for some of his people who were in a state of dire need. And this necessity was caused by overcrowding on barren mountain sides.[1]

Had this policy of eviction been carried out in the Ulster settlements, the people would have risen in rebellion. An Ulster farmer told me this, and I have no reason for doubting his word. Ulster men rose in rebellion at the end of last century for much less cause.[2]

Any person wishing to study further the history of clearances of good districts and the overcrowding of bad, might read the " Westmeath Act," one of the most stringent ever passed in any country. In this county may be seen the effects of the system of which I have tried to give some account. And it was here that some of the greatest crimes were committed. The great severity of the Act was the outcome of the shocking state of society, caused in an Irish county by a selfish and heartless policy.

These poor peasants living in overcrowded districts are common to all or nearly all great estates. The next common characteristic is the " agent." This great personage, like the country in which he lives, varies greatly. Sometimes he is an ex-military or militia officer, habits of command, and an imposing presence, being thought useful by some landlords. The agent is sometimes a connection of the noble owner, and very often he is the son of an agent, the calling being hereditary in certain families. He is looked upon as the representative of the landlord

[1] Kilcoo, Bryansford, County Down.
[2] See appendix I.

during the absence of the latter—this period usually
varying from the entire year, to the greater portion
of it. As the Lord-Lieutenant of Ireland is to royalty
so is the Irish agent to his employer. The agent is a
justice of the peace, a grand juror, and often chairman
of the Board of Guardians. And on very large and
scattered estates, where there are two or more agents,
these are all in the beforenamed posts of authority.
But of late years the agent has lost much of his
dignity. " Popular " appointments to the commission of
the peace have crowded him off the bench of justice.
And the farmers, being independent since the passing
of the Land Acts, elect men of their own class as
chairmen of Boards of Guardians.

Still, the agent has some power left : rents, particularly in bad times, cannot be punctually paid, and then
the farmer is much at the agent's mercy. Land Acts
do not apply to town holdings, and thus the shopkeeper and townsman is as much subject to the
agent's authority as ever. This authority is called the
" office." It is there rents are paid, and from thence
all mandates are sent forth. The landlord is generally
unknown personally to his tenants. They know his
name, and that is all.

Sometimes the agent lives in the family mansion ;
oftener a new house has been built for him at great
cost, or a residence in the neighbourhood bought or
rented for him. He is also highly paid, and in every
respect the dignity of his position is taken into account. There are one or more clerks in the office,
and a number of bailiffs are scattered over the estate.
The chief clerk or head bailiff is often a sort of under-

agent, doing most of the "work," such as it is. This work almost altogether consists in the collecting of rents. Improvements, such as building and draining, are nearly always made by the tenants, who also farm as they like. The office has nothing to do with such things. The bailiffs "warn" or tell the tenants to pay the rent, and the clerks keep books in which the payments are entered. What the agent does, except "awe the crowd" by his stately demeanour, it would be difficult to say. These, of course, are the very greatest agents; but when the estate is poor or the owner needy, the agent is not so highly paid or luxuriously lodged. In these cases he is often a civil, business-like person, striving to make the most of the property under his charge, *i.e.*, to get as much rent as he can out of it. Men of this sort are often very unpopular, as they are frequently obliged to put the "screw on." When an estate is in Chancery, a "receiver" is appointed : this is usually a land-agent or person of that class. When estates are not very large the same agent acts for several landlords. New owners, particularly business men and lawyers, have agents of a humble sort, like bailiffs or tax-gatherers, and sometimes a clerk from the owner's office collects the rents.

In talking with the people, I have always heard them speak in bitter terms of the luxurious abode and style of living of the "great agent." They seemed to think that rents, paid often with great difficulty, should not be spent in keeping a mere servant in such state. Certainly the new owners were able to get their rents paid quite as well as, or better, than those of the great landlord, to a common agent or clerk.

These small holders and great land-agents are the two chief features of Irish rural society. The great numbers of the one class, and the high authority of the other, attract notice, and everyone hears or knows something about either. But there are several other classes of persons who live on estates great and small, and who, though insignificant in numbers, are by no means so in other respects. There is to begin with the comfortable peasant, or farmer, as he is called. I have already described this person as he is to be found in Ulster. The comfortable farmer of other parts of Ireland differs from the Ulsterman, chiefly as to the appearance of his farm and homestead; it has a comparatively untidy and unthrifty look, and the house is often built of mud and thatched. This is easily accounted for by the want of security all over every part of Ireland, parts of Ulster excepted. Until of late years, the Leinster or Munster farmer could be ejected without getting the smallest compensation. Under such circumstances he could scarcely be expected to improve his farm or dwelling. Notwithstanding the aspect of their farms, these men are often well off. On nearly everything, religion excepted, they think with their fellow-peasants in Ulster. There is the same common hostility to the landlord, it being quite a mistake to suppose that the Protestant tenantry of Ulster are better disposed towards their landlords than tenants in most other parts of Ireland. They are more shrewd and sensible, as well as being better educated, and therefore do not act so foolishly as their class elsewhere in Ireland. But the desire to get rid of the landlord on the easiest possible terms is common to all Irish peasants. This sentiment has grown greatly of late years. The anti-landlord feeling is equally strong against all proprietors of every class and every creed. Much has been said as to landlords of "alien race and faith" being the cause of Irish discontent; race or faith of the landlord has nothing to do with the bad feeling on the side of the tenant. On the contrary, the most unpopular landlords have been of the same faith as their tenants. This has been the case both in Ulster and in other parts of Ireland.[1] The reports of cases in the land courts and the general history of the past few years will bear out this statement.

As to the nature of the terms on which the landlord is to be got rid of, North and South differ but little. If the facts of tenant-right and easier rents for the last century or two are taken into account, Ulster farmers are more unreasonable than those elsewhere. I remember once hearing a man considered to be a very respectable farmer, and a "Protestant," laying down the lines of a "fair settlement" between landlord and tenant. These were "that rents were first to be considerably lowered, and that these reduced rents were only to be paid during the life-time of the landlord." After his death land was to be "free." As this person's landlord was an elderly man who had served in the Crimea, and had suffered much from what he had undergone, the tenant would not have had long to wait for his "free land." These ideas are those of

---

[1] Lord Kenmare, Mr. D'La Poer, and others in the south of Ireland, have had, as all newspaper readers must be aware, much trouble with their tenantry.

a great number of what are considered to be "moderate men" in many localities in Ulster. In most parts of Ireland the tenants are willing to buy their farms, under recent Acts, on terms quite as just as those in Ulster. If there is any difference, it is rather against the Ulstermen. But as every person who has dealings with Ulster must know, the standard of business morality in that province is a very low one.

In every part of Ireland the peasant is a man long settled in his farm, and from different reasons, looking upon it as his own. He is called a "farmer," but he is not such in the strict sense of the word, at least, as it is understood in most parts of the British Isles. But there are in Ireland a few tenant farmers in the ordinary sense of the word. These are men who rented land from year to year, or on twenty-one or thirty-one year leases. They were looked on as not having any interest in their holdings, and were moved to other farms or ejected without any stir being caused thereby. The peasantry looked on them as interlopers, and showed little sympathy with them when they were ill-used. Sometimes the landlords built houses on these farms, charging interest in the form of rent. Sometimes the tenant made the best of the hovels to be found on the land, and which had been built by people who were evicted at some former time. There was no need to make these tenants forego any claim for compensation formerly. But after the first Land Act, they became entitled to be paid for their improvements, and leases were then made in which the tenant bound himself not to set up any claim at the end of the term. Previous to the passing of this Act, some Ulster tenants who had made all improvements themselves under the "custom" took out leases. It was said by some persons that pressure had been applied by the landlords to make them do so. Be this as it may, when the tenant-right custom was legalised, these leaseholders found themselves excepted. Instead of having a property in their farms, they had merely leases for short terms at a full rent. And when rents were lowered by the land courts, the leaseholders could not go into "court."[1] They were bound by their leases to pay rents now much too high. At length, by recent enactments, all Irish tenants are put on the same footing, have fixed interests in their farms, and can get their rents settled in the land courts. Many people have complained of this, and stated that men who paid nothing for the "good-will" of their farms should not have fixed interests conferred on them. There may be some slight injustice done, but, on the whole, the leaseholder has a just claim to the benefits he has received. These enactments merely apply to tillage farms; land let for grazing purposes only is excepted from their operation.

These farmers above-named have usually good-sized farms, often as much as three or four hundred acres. These holdings are usually well-tilled, but from the want of trees and hedges, often do not look very well. The farms are mostly in the eastern and north-eastern parts of Ireland, where the country is bare and ugly. The fields are often divided by furze fences or open drains, and this gives the country a

[1] See appendix J.

ragged and poor appearance. Notwithstanding this,
the country is fertile and grows good crops of wheat
and potatoes, though for the greater part it is unsuited for grazing.

Unless where these men have very old leases at
low rents they are not well off. Labour in eastern
Ireland is quite as dear as in many English agricultural counties, and prices of all kinds of farm produce
are lower than in England. Besides this, the rents of
these farms have not been greatly lowered. When
all the facts are taken into account, it will be found
that farmers of this class are very heavily weighted.
They live comfortably enough, drive jaunting-cars,
and wear good clothes on Sundays, but it is often a
struggle to keep out of bankruptcy, and farmers' sons
and daughters often work hard enough in the fields.
In some instances farmers of this class have bene-
fited very much by recent legislation, getting as much
as thirty per cent. off their rents. But most of them
have not got so much; besides that, the price of grain
has fallen greatly since the rents were fixed. Farmers
say that they are not so well off as formerly, and that
the fall in the price of farm produce has counterbalanced the fall in rents.

Another occupier of land is the big grazier or land-
grabber. These are to be found in the parts of Ireland
that are suited for grazing purposes. Though the
number of these men is few, their acres are many. I
have known of cattle kings who had several thousand
acres of grazing land, a farm here, and a farm there.
They are of all sizes, from two or three hundred acres
upwards. Cattle salesmen in Dublin, the market, gen-

erally hold quantities of grass land. There are also cattle-dealers who have grass farms, and there are graziers who cannot be termed dealers or jobbers. These latter buy stock from the peasant who raises it, or from other graziers. Some keep only store or lean cattle, others who have rich land fatten large beasts. Some graze sheep, others graze both sheep and cattle. They keep the kind of stock that suits their land. These are looked after by a few herdsmen, ill-clad, poorly paid, and living in hovels that are a disgrace to Christendom.

Another person who usually holds under some great landowner is the "for ever" men or long leaseholder. This is his northern title, but he has different others. Sometimes he is called a "half sir," "half gentleman," or gentleman, according to the size of his property. He holds by a tenure almost if not quite peculiar to Ireland. This is a lease of lives renewable for ever now often converted into a "fee farm grant." In the north of Ireland he holds often but a few acres of land, but, as a rule, over the country he has two or three hundred acres at a low rent, frequently but half-a-crown an acre. He is nearly always of English or Scotch origin. The origin of freeholds, or long leases at nominal rents, is various. In one very remarkable case in Ulster, a number of long leaseholds were created of all sizes from a few acres to two or three hundred in a very simple way. The landlord was in a position to make these grants, which he did over a very great extent of property. A grant was made to any tenant who could pay down a lump sum. Whether the tenants had the money or whether they

G

borrowed it cannot now be known, but most of the estate was let on long terms at nominal rents. On it may now be seen very comfortable dwellings and good farm buildings. It is a standing proof of the fact that security of tenure encourages thrift, and also constitutes a strong argument in favour of a peasant proprietary. As a rule the long leaseholder, or freeholder, is of much more ancient date than any of these last-named landholders. He is usually scattered up and down, singly or in very small numbers. These grants may have often been for some service rendered to the landlord in former times.

This is a brief account of most of the occupiers of land in Ireland. There are a few others who hold land but are chiefly engaged in business of some sort. Shopkeepers and publicans often have farms or a few fields, and dealers nearly all hold land, from a small field held by a petty jobber, to a large farm occupied by a big cow-jobber. In some parts of Ireland, round villages and small towns, are a number of little fields held by villagers and townsmen at very high rents. These are called (humorously, I suppose) "town parks." Anything less like parks could scarcely be. They are excepted from the operation of the Land Acts, and as a result the villagers pay dearly for their "bits of ground."

It would be impossible to find specimens of all these classes of landholders or occupiers on any one estate. As before-mentioned, the agents and the peasants are the only people common to all great estates. As a rule the territorial estate is held partly by small holders, and partly by a larger class of tenants. The latter may be graziers, or large farmers, or rich peasants, or freeholders, but seldom or never all four.

A very common sort of property in Ireland is an estate on which there is, first, a great mansion. This is always on a very large scale, rarely ancient, and usually dating from the last century or beginning of this. There are some old castles, which have been restored and fitted up to suit modern needs, but they are few and far between. Surrounding the house or castle is a large park, or, as it is called in Ireland, a "demesne." These parks sometimes are thousands of acres in extent. Adjoining the demesne, which is often walled in, is the village or town. This is sometimes well cared for, but much oftener falling into decay. Village and demesne are in the best part of the estate, which extends for many miles around. This best part may be held by large holders, or it may be all in the hands of the peasantry. As a rule it is held by graziers or large farmers, it being the general policy to crowd the peasantry on to the mountainous or bad parts of the estate. There they are out of sight of the visitors, who from time to time may accompany the landlord when he comes to his "place in Ireland." On many properties no pretence is made of keeping up appearances, and things look as bad near the mansion and village as anywhere else. The greater part of some large estates are in the hands of good tenants, but on others there are very few. Subdivision on some estates has done much mischief, great areas of country being covered with struggling peasants trying to exist on small patches of bad land. Much of the misery of Ireland is to be found on great territorial estates, and some of these have become historical of late years.[1] This unhappy state of things is greatly the result of neglect on the part of both owners and agents for the last century. It would be difficult to find such a " damnosa hereditas" as some of these estates now are.

The estates of the smaller landowners are very different from one another. Some are parts of great estates broken up after the famine, and sold in lots. On these there is seldom a park or mansion. There are a certain number of tenants, some good and some bad. There may be a part let to a large grazier, and part to a few small poor occupiers. Or the property may all be let to well-to-do peasants, with fair-sized tillage farms. Where the lot containing the mansion has been sold to a grazier or non-resident, the house has been allowed to fall into decay. It is melancholy in some parts of Ireland to see fine old mansions falling into ruin, sometimes occupied as tenements by poor families, who stuff rags into the broken windows.

There are very few resident gentry in Ireland as a rule. New owners, whether business men or graziers, seldom have residences on their properties, and, when they have, do not usually live in them. Those landowners of any extent who can afford to do so generally live in England or abroad. Others live on the Continent from motives of economy. The residents are generally people fond of a little sport, which can be

---

[1] Clanricarde, Kenmare, and Lansdowne estates have all been made the objects of much controversy.

had cheaply in Ireland, or else penurious men who hold part of their property in their own hands, and look after all their own affairs. These two last-named classes often belong to the old families, and have a sort of attachment to their places. The latter are usually large, with houses out of proportion to the size of the estate. From either inability to do so or penuriousness, these houses and parks are seldom well kept. Men of this sort become scarcer each year. Their influence has declined from various causes, and sport becomes more difficult to get. Hunting has been objected to by the tenants in many places, and game preservation is difficult in the face of popular opposition. Indeed, game of some kinds threaten to become extinct in Ireland. In some ways these resident landowners will be a loss to the country. Hunting tends to improve the breed of horses, and in following the sport landlords and tenants are apt to get on good terms with each other. But the sporting characteristics of the Irishman are fast becoming things of the past; his tastes instead are becoming political.

There are a new class of landowners now coming to the front—that is, those tenants who have bought their farms under recent Purchase Acts. It is yet too soon to form an opinion of these new landowners, but there is every reason to hope that they will become a useful class of men. So far, they have honestly paid their instalments of interest and purchase-money, and seem likely to do so in the future.[1] In few European countries has there been greater need of

[1] See Parliamentary returns of Land Purchase Acts,

a class such as this, as in Ireland. If they become numerous enough they may be the means of saving their country from much social disorder.

It cannot be denied that there is much that is dangerous to society in the present state of Ireland. The only means of remedying this state of things is the creation of a great number of proprietors, each having a certain stake in the country. Men of this class have been the means of saving society on the continent of Europe, and may yet do so in Ireland.

# CHAPTER VII.

## THE IRISH LABOURER.

THE Irish labourer has been called a "farmer who has not got a farm." This is true to a very limited extent. There are a class of small holders in the far west of Ireland, who are farmers of a sort on their miserable patches in the winter and spring, and are labourers on English farms during the harvest-time. A man of this class who happens not to have a farm of his own is "a farmer without a farm," but most Irish harvestmen have patches of land, however small. In fact, the poor western peasant may be looked on as the connecting link between the "small holder" and the labourer in the proper sense of the word. But it is a sad fact that these connecting links may be found in the poor and mountainous districts all over Ireland.

The labourer or "labouring boy," that is, the man who has no land and earns a living by unskilled labour, belongs to a class small in Ireland as compared with other parts of the British Isles. Labourers in Ireland are comparatively scarce, because of the number of peasant holdings, worked by the occupiers, large grass farms, the fewness of towns, and the want of trade. And from this latter cause there are numbers of unemployed or half-employed men in the southern towns who are dangerous more or less to society.

There are two sorts of Irish labourers; first, those who

work on railways or public works, or in corn-mills, or
on quays or wharves, or at any kind of work which
calls for a certain amount of bodily strength. These
men are sometimes the sons of peasants or small
farmers, and sometimes the offspring of tradesmen or
labourers. Such men usually earn good wages. These
vary somewhat in different localities, the wages in the
North being much higher than those in the South.
But the strong Irishman is always fairly paid, because,
if he cannot get what he considers enough at home,
he can always command good wages in the English
towns. The cost of living being cheaper at home, he
will work for less wages in Ireland than in England.
This class of men is usually to be found in those districts where there is an admixture of Teutonic blood,
which is the case in most parts of Ulster and Leinster,
and in a part of Munster. These strong labourers get
fewer and fewer every year; such men are in too great
demand abroad to rest contented with the wages to be
had in their own country. Every farmer in the tillage districts makes the same complaint, i.e., "dearness
and scarcity of labour." This means occasional labour,
for labourers of this class do not like to hire as farm
servants; they only work for the farmers at harvest
time, or when labour of other sorts fails. But these
men now leave home often as soon as they are grown
up. Public work on railways and roads is ill-paid in
Ireland, hence, contractors have now often to be content with men of poor physique. "Good men," i.e.,
strong men, are seldom to be found now unless about
wharves or quays or in breweries, or such places where
they can earn good wages.

In poor localities labour is cheap and plentiful, and all kinds of public works, such as new roads or harbours, are hailed as unmixed blessings. In well-to-do places it is otherwise ; labour is difficult to get and men have to be brought from other districts. A dispensary or Poor Law doctor complained lately that he had to attend, gratis, on five hundred men who had been imported into his district from other places to do certain public work.[1] These sort of men are brought from poor districts in the south and west, and from different causes are not of good physique. They are active and hardy, and do well enough for common sorts of labour and for harvesting. The harvestmen are usually of this kind of physique, and during the greater part of the year, when they are at home, are thankful to obtain any sort of employment; as their little patches of land are not enough to fully occupy their time.

In the good parts of Ulster there is a class of labourers almost peculiar to those districts. They are called "cottars," and rent a house yearly or half-yearly from a farmer, who usually bargains that the cottar shall work for a certain number of days in harvest-time, at the current rate of wages. The cottar, on his side, bargains that the farmer shall plant a certain quantity of potatoes for him, or give him ground which he can plant for himself. He has generally a pig and some fowls, so that potatoes are absolutely needful. The "cottar house" is far better than the common Irish cabin. It is built of stone with a chimney at either end. There are two apart-

[1] *Irish Times,* January, 1892.

ments, one on either side of the door, and a window with sashes in each room. Sometimes these sashes open, but, as a rule, they do not. A continued war goes on between the farmer and the cottar about the roof; this is generally thatched, and often in bad repair. The farmer wants all his straw for his cattle, and is slow to mend the roof of the cottar house. As the cottar family often do a little weaving or embroidery, locally called "flowering," they are annoyed at the rain coming through the roof and spoiling their work, hence, the squabbling and bickering. Though these houses are solid and often well-built, they are generally in bad repair. Inside, they are nearly always clean, but the outside has often a very bad appearance. If the farmers will not or cannot keep them in a good state, it might be thought that the landlord or agent would do something, if only for the credit of the estate. But the agent seems to think it to be no part of his duty to look after such "common, vulgar folk," and the absentee landlord knows or cares nothing about them. It is often pitiable to see decent, poor people trying to make the best of their miserable dwellings.

The cottar works in the winter time in the small oat and flax scutching-mills, which are to be found on the banks of every stream in rural Ulster. Here, he earns good wages. In the summer time when the streams run low and the mills are stopped, he works for the farmers, or on the roads, or at anything he can get to do. Work of some kind or another is always to be had in these districts. The cottar is usually a man of good physique, he is tolerably fed in his youth, and is of pure Teutonic blood as a rule.

Were it not for the mills, and the semi-independent arrangement he makes with the farmer, the cottar would long ago have been an extinct species. As it is, he is to be found in much smaller numbers than formerly. Comfortable as those men are compared with their brethren in other parts of Ireland, there is yet a constant emigration going on. The reason is the same, the great demand for strong men in England and the colonies.

None of the foregoing kinds of labourers are to be confounded with the farm labourer or " servant boy," who is quite a different sort of person. He is much less independent, as he is merely a servant, often hired half-yearly, and prosecuted if he leaves his employment before his time is up. There are two kinds of farm servants, one, who is usually hired half-yearly, gets bed and board in the farm-house, and a half-yearly wage as well. These are generally boys of from sixteen to eighteen, or young, unmarried men. The other kind of farm servant is always a married man, and lives in a village, or on the farm where he is employed. In some districts the men live chiefly in villages, going some distance to their work every day. Their lot is a wretched one, living in a cabin in a village street. This hovel is ill-kept, ill-drained, with a roof of rotten thatch, from which the green ooze drains down the walls. These men have no land, no pig, no poultry. They have miserable wages and everything must be bought. Everything means some potatoes, a little bad bread, stuff called tea, and perhaps a bit of coarse, American bacon on Sundays.

When the labourer lives on the farm, miserable
though his dwelling is, he is better off than in the
village. In the first place, there is fresh air around
the cabin. In the next place, the labourer can keep a
few fowls, and, what is of still greater consequence,
can often get some milk for his family. In this
respect Irish farmers treat their men better than
English labourers are treated. In England the
labourer can rarely or never get milk from his employer. In Ireland he often can get some milk, it is
not the best, being what is called skimmed milk, and
sometimes only buttermilk, still these are better than
nothing. Twopence a quart for good milk is a common price in rural Ireland, so that it is within the
reach of poor people. The small farmers or peasants
are generally willing to sell milk at this rate to the
labouring classes.

One of the great reasons for the good physique of
the Irish labourer is, that in his boyhood he can
generally get some milk. In many parts of rural
England children are brought up without, or nearly
without, milk.

Labourers' dwellings in Ireland are usually cabins
of the most miserable kind, the worst hovels being
often in the best parts of the country. It is a common
thing to find a man, his wife, and several children
living in a hovel with but one room. In this apartment the family all eat and drink and sleep, and its
atmosphere is often very bad. Mud houses are said
to be warm, as no air gets through, and the window
is generally a single pane built into the mud wall.
The atmosphere of such a dwelling, with, perhaps,

ten persons sleeping in a space a few yards square, may be more easily imagined than described. Were it not that these people spend most of their lives in the open air, existence would be impossible.

Though the "cottar house" of Ulster is comfortable enough, the dwellings of the farm servants are little, if anything, better than those elsewhere. I have seen on large Ulster farms, on which there were good slated houses and farm buildings, the most wretched hovels. On a "for ever" large farm, belonging to a man in business rich enough to build a "ballroom" to his house, were three or four cabins no better than those elsewhere in Ireland. These dwellings were dirty and ill-kept, and their appearance was a blot on the landscape. All over great estates, where the farms are large and the houses good, are hidden away groups of hovels which are unfit for human dwellings. They are low, cramped, and dirty, being frequently situated in unhealthy places where the drainage is bad. I have seen on a farm in one of the best parts of Ulster, two one-roomed hovels; the windows did not open, and one cabin had no chimney. In one of these lived a woman with three or four children. In the other lived a man with a wife and family. Outside, the houses were dirty and in bad repair; inside the occupants tried to keep things clean. What a struggle this was may be imagined from the facts of beds, chairs, table, and cooking utensils being all stowed in a space about the size of a small attic.

Landlords will sometimes help tenants to build farmhouses and steadings, giving slates and timber, which are arranged for either in the rent or price of the tenant-right. Yet on these farms are filthy huts, which are quite neglected, though why, if only for appearance sake, something is not done, is a puzzle. Many of these estates are shown to visitors, and the good farmhouses pointed out as proofs of the excellence of the landlord. But if the hovels in the out-of-the-way places were also seen, these visitors might go away with a very different impression of the "splendidly managed Ulster estate."

These miserable labourers' cabins are usually found on large tillage farms in eastern and north-eastern Ireland as well as in the grazing districts. It is in the latter that the Irish mud cabin is to be found at its worst. So far as I have seen, the worst, dirtiest, and most unhealthy hovels have been in the best parts of Ireland. Where the farms are small, in what have been called "peasant districts," labourers are scarcely to be found. Though many of the peasants' dwellings are poor enough, none I have seen are so bad as the hovels of the labourers. Large farms, grazing or tillage, in Ireland nearly always mean squalid villages and miserable cabins.

According to recent enactments, Boards of Guardians are empowered to borrow money from the State at the rate of four per cent., this money to be used for the purpose of building labourers' dwellings. This rate of four per cent. pays off both principal and interest after a certain number of years. The cottages have, or are to have, half an acre of land attached,—the weekly rent of land and cottage is one shilling.[1] In some few places these Acts have been put in force, but in those districts in which they are most needed

[1] Labourers' Dwellings Acts—the first passed in 1883.

they have not. It is very difficult to discover the real reasons for this. One reason is that the shilling a-week is said not to be punctually paid, and that if it was, it would nothing like pay the interest on the outlay. The result is, that the rates must be charged with the interest on the borrowed sum. This, under the system of rating by electoral divisions, would greatly raise the rates. As the Guardians are chiefly tenant farmers they object to this, especially where the farms are large and the payments would be greater. Yet these are just the districts where new cottages are needed, as labourers are most numerous in such localities. Though the first of these Acts was passed nearly ten years ago, there are districts in the east and north-east of Ireland where they have never been put in force. The one-roomed hovels to be found in some of these places are a disgrace to humanity. Yet there they remain, as well as rows of mud cabins very little better, and all this within easy reach of the metropolis. In many distant parts of the country, cottages have been built under the Acts, the Guardians and ratepayers being probably persons either not paying many rates or not caring. In these localities it is said "that the people don't like the houses, and say that good cabins would be more comfortable."

Labour is, as a rule, in good demand in most parts of Ireland, the exceptions being found either in the poor districts of the far south and west, or in the rich grazing parts of the island. In the former localities, the labourer, in the strict sense of the word, is scarcely to be found, but the small holders would be often glad to get employment. This is especially

the case in bad seasons or during the partial visitations
of famine to which these districts are subject.

In the grass countries the condition of the poorer
classes is a very miserable one, perhaps worse than
elsewhere in Ireland, and this despite the fact that
the landholders are richer and the rural population
smaller than in any other part of Ireland. I remember
once being in a "grass country" not far from the
metropolis. The land for some distance round about
where I stood was in the hands of one mammoth
grazier. Here and there scattered over the country
were mud cabins, all inhabited by very poor people.
There being neither woods nor bogs, these people had
no fuel except cow-dung dried in the sun. The land
was much too precious to allow of the smallest scrap
of potato-ground. Some of the men were employed
as herdsmen, others had but occasional jobs, others
dragged out existence, no one seemed to know how.
All the children were nearly naked and some of them
begged for "coppers."

A northern cattle-dealer once said to me: "The big
gentlemen and graziers up in Meath ought to be
ashamed of themselves. If you go into a poor man's
house to light your pipe, you find neither light nor
fire nor food in the place." Anyone passing through
the grass districts may see these miserable cabins by
the roadsides. He will also pass through very poor
villages, chiefly made up of mud cabins; and many
wonder how the inhabitants find employment. The
country is all in grass, and there is neither tillage,
farming, trade, nor business of any kind. Herding
cattle, driving them to market or fair, and occasional

work on the roads afford some employment, and may
serve to keep the people from starving altogether.
Many also engage in the trade of begging, the beggar
locking up his or her cabin and ranging far and near
in search of alms.

The want of fuel adds greatly to the misery of
these people ; bogs are hardly to be found in these
districts, and dried cow-dung forms a poor substitute
for peat or "turf." Coal is quite too dear, as it
has to be brought for some distance from the
nearest seaport. Milk is also scarce, the grass
being used for feeding or fattening and not for dairy
purposes. A herdsman is often allowed the grazing
of a cow as part of his wages, but he cannot always
afford to buy one. The want of fuel or milk, the
miserable cabins built of mud, in bad repair, and
reeking with filth, often with but one apartment, the
want of employment, and low rate of wages, all these
circumstances combine to make the condition of the
population of the grass countries a miserable one.
And it is to be borne in mind that the landowners
and graziers of these parts of Ireland are rich men,
well able to afford good wages, and to build comfortable cottages for the people.

Labourers' wages are better than their dwellings.
In most fairly good tillage districts in Ireland twelve
shillings a-week, or two shillings a-day, is the usual rate.
In remote parts of the country wages are less than these ;
in parts of the west they are nine shillings a-week in winter and ten in summer. In west Cork, near Skibbereen,
they are as low as nine shillings a-week, or eighteen-
pence a-day at all times, harvest perhaps excepted.

H

These wages are those paid without extras or per-quisites of any kind; with these, the cash payments become lower. Five and six shillings a-week with "diet"[1] are common rates. Farm servants boarded and lodged in farmhouses are paid half-yearly some-times five, sometimes eight pounds, according to the locality.

Some time ago a public personage visiting Ireland spoke of labourers having but six shillings a-week.[2] His examples were drawn from the county of Cork. Careful inquiry being made in the county, no rates lower than nine shillings a-week can be discovered. Of course there are labourers who get but six shillings a-week with "diet," or there may be those who have perquisites or allowances along with that sum, or it may be paid to old or decrepit men, or to boys of fourteen or fifteen years of age. But no district can be found where the average wages of able-bodied labourers are but six shillings a-week and no other allowance. The lowest rate I have heard of was in the county of Meath, where a herdsman was said to have had but seven shillings a-week and a free house or rather hovel.

In the good Ulster districts wages are much better than those in other parts of Ireland, twelve shillings a-week, with a free house and a certain quantity of potatoes planted and worked by the farmer, are com-mon rates of payment. Fourteen shillings a-week and a free house are also common. But, as a rule,

[1] "Diet" means that the labourer gets his meals from his employer.

[2] Sir John Gorst.

labourers prefer less wages, and allowances of potato-ground or other matters, as most of them keep pigs. Good labourers are generally considered to be worth fourteen or fifteen shillings a-week.

Nothing is to be gained by overstating a case, or by quoting an exceptional instance, as a type of a whole. Statements of this sort are certain to be shown up, and the cause in which they are professedly made is injured thereby. Now, the case of the Irish labourer is on the whole one that calls for much sym-pathy, and cannot afford to be injured by rash or sham advocates. His grievances are not so much the rate of wages paid, as the shameful manner in which he is housed, and the great want of employment in the grazing and remote districts.

If the average rate of wages paid in Ireland is com-pared, first, with the rates paid in southern and eastern English counties, and next, if the average prices of food, such as potatoes, meal, eggs, butter, in Ireland are compared with those in England, it will be found that there is not much to choose between the condition of the Irish and English labourer so far as payment goes. In the east and south of England there are villages where the labourers are stated, on good authority, not to get more than from ten to twelve shillings a-week.[1] If the purchasing power of nine shillings a-week in West Cork is compared with that of ten or eleven in certain English counties, it will be found that the labourer is equally badly off in each. The Irish labourer is much worse housed, but then he

---

[1] Suffolk, Dorset, and others.

pays less for his cabin than the Englishman pays for
his cottage, and can usually keep a pig, which the
latter is not often allowed to do.  This must not be
taken as stating that because the Irish labourer is no
worse paid than his English brother, that therefore he
should be content.  The fact is that the condition of
each is deplorable in this respect, and that both have
a common ground of complaint.

The bad housing and want of employment in certain districts are the Irish labourers real troubles.  In
both of these respects the labourers in some parts of
Ireland are much worse off than those in any part of
England.  As I have tried to show, no people in Ireland are worse off than the poor of the " grass countries."  From the want of any tillage, trade, or other
means of employment, the " big men " can grind down
the poor to a starvation rate of wage.  And the want
of fuel, milk, or potato-ground is also a serious one.
In short, the labourer of the Irish grazing districts
suffers from all the drawbacks of the poorest Irish
and English localities combined.  He gets the lowest
Irish rate of payment, and is without the benefits,
such as cheap turf, milk, and other things, which
might, to a certain extent, make up for these small
wages.

The Irish labourer is, as a rule, very ignorant.
This, coupled with the fact of his miserable state,
makes him the prey of unprincipled people.  He has
often been drawn into taking part in certain movements, for which he has been severely punished,
whilst those who have hounded him on, have escaped
scot free.  Many public persons, whether so-called

" patriots " or "loyalists," talk loudly of "heading in-
surrections," or "taking up arms," if certain things
are done or not done by the ruling powers. This kind
of talk is the grossest " bunkum," and deceives no
well-informed person. But, unhappily, it is otherwise
with the ignorant. How many poor Irishmen both in
the north and south have been shot down, or ruined
for life, by listening to the advice of unprincipled
" spouters," who have always taken good care to save
their own persons.

Out of north-eastern Ulster the labourers are not
numerous as compared with the rest of the population ; but in the manufacturing and some agricultural
parts of the North working-men form a very considerable proportion of the inhabitants. They have no
idea of combining in any societies for their common
good. Differences of race, or, as it is called, "religion,"
keep them asunder. These differences have always
been fomented by employers and estate " offices," and
the richer classes have thriven by the quarrels of
those in their employment. The men have been
quite too busy in contending with each other to think
of combining in order to better their condition.
The loss of life during the last ten years in these
party riots has been very great, not to speak of other
evils resulting therefrom. There has been a state of
things in parts of Ulster almost without parallel in
Europe, and those who should act as peacemakers
pursue a contrary course of action. That large employers should, in some cases, be members of certain
societies, and in others be large subscribers to them,
is much to their discredit. The reason for this policy

may be found in the fact that party riots tend to keep
wages low and profits high.[1]

There has been much talk of late in Ulster of arm-
ing and turning out in battle should certain legisla-
tive changes take place. The people who are to turn
out must be those chiefly of the working-class, as the
militia regiments are recruited from them, and, with
some army reserve men, they are the only people in
the North who have any military training. Now,
without expressing any opinion as to the constitu-
tional alterations that are proposed, it may be stated
safely that a greater piece of wickedness and folly
than this talked of "turn-out" could scarcely be. For
the result would be that English troops would be
called out to put down the insurrection, that a fearful
quantity of blood would be shed, and many widows
and orphans be made. And not only this, but the
country would be ravaged, homesteads burnt, and
outrages perpetrated by the soldiery. Another thing
may be stated with equal certainty, and that is, that
the rich men who encourage this notion, and who may
perhaps subscribe something for arms, will be the first
to flee across the Channel and disclaim all connection
with the rising. As has happened before in Ireland,
the working-class and the peasantry will be the
sufferers, and those who incite to rebel will escape.[2]

[1] The wages of grown-up persons working in spinning mills
near, or in, Belfast, are said on good authority to be as low as six
shillings a-week, with no extras. See appendix K.

[2] See appendix L.

# CHAPTER VIII.

## IRISH EDUCATION.

THE present system of National Education in Ireland was founded in 1831. In this year grants of public money for the education of the poor were entrusted to the lord-lieutenant in order that they might be applied to the education of the people. This education was to be given to children of every religious belief, and to be superintended by commissioners appointed for the purpose. The great principle on which the system was founded was that of " united secular and separate religious instruction." No child should be required to attend any religious instruction which should be contrary to the wishes of his or her parents or guardians. Times were to be set apart during which children were to have such religious instruction as their parents might think proper. It was to be the duty of the Commissioners to see that these principles were carried out and not infringed on in any way. They had also power to give or refuse money to those who applied for aid to build schools.

Schools are "vested" and "non-vested." Vested schools are those built by the Board or National Education ; non-vested schools are the ordinary schools, and are managed by those who built them. If a committee of persons build a school, it is looked on by the Board as the "patron." If a landowner or private person builds a school, he is regarded as the patron if he has no committee. The patron, whether landlord or committee, has power to appoint or dismiss a manager, who corresponds with the Board. The manager is also responsible for the due or thorough observance of the laws and rules. Teachers are paid by him after he certifies that the laws have been kept, and gives the attendance for each quarter. When an individual is patron, he may appoint himself manager, and thus fill both offices. The patron, if not himself manager, is bound, with the manager, to keep the school premises in good repair, and to see that books and requisites are supplied. It is the duty of the manager to oversee the teaching, to give directions to the teachers, and to sign agreements with them when they are appointed. He can also appoint and dismiss the teachers, but often does it along with the patron, giving the teachers three months' notice.

The ordinary or non-vested schools can at any time be withdrawn from the control of the Board of Commissioners of National Education. Most schools are built by local persons and are often very mean structures, as the people fear sometimes that the attendance may fall under thirty, in which event the grant will be withdrawn and the house thus become useless. The Board gives a grant if the district requires a house; in this event it retains the deed, and on complaint being made may prevent religious meetings being held in the school.

If a sectarian school be placed under the control of the Board, it will recognise the person who applies to have the school under the Board as the manager. But a notice must be put up to the effect that the school is a national one, and religious instruction can only be given at stated times, when those pupils, who dislike it, may withdraw.

The teachers are paid by salaries and by results fees. The Boards of Guardians have power to contribute to these results fees. Some unions do so and are called " contributory."

School managers in Ireland are nearly always clerics of some denomination. There are sometimes, but very rarely, lay managers. Persons not of the religion of the manager often complain of a sectarian atmosphere in the national school.

Whether the Irish people themselves do not care for having their children well taught, or whether those set over them are careless on the matter, the fact remains that the Irish people are ignorant compared with those of other countries. From the census returns of 1881 it appears that but fifty-nine per cent. of the people of Ireland are able to read and write.

The greater number of national schools throughout Ireland are what are called " unmixed," that is, attended by children of one denomination only. The rest of the schools are called " mixed," that is, attended by children of different forms of religion. The percentage of schools that show a " mixed " attendance tends to become smaller each year, as may be seen from the subjoined table :—

| | 1881 | 1882 | 1883 | 1884 | 1885 | 1886 | 1887 | 1888 | 1839 | 1890 |
|---|---|---|---|---|---|---|---|---|---|---|
| Ulster, ...... | 75·0 | 73·7 | 73·3 | 72·1 | 70·0 | 67·5 | 65·7 | 64·5 | 63·6 | 62·8 |
| Munster, .... | 39·7 | 37·7 | 37·4 | 36·7 | 36·3 | 36·3 | 35·3 | 34·3 | 33·3 | 32·9 |
| Leinster,..... | 46·7 | 47·1 | 47·8 | 44·8 | 46·9 | 44·6 | 45·9 | 45·7 | 44·4 | 43·2 |
| Connaught,.. | 43·7 | 42·5 | 42·0 | 40·9 | 38 4 | 39·2 | 38·4 | 37·0 | 36·6 | 36·4 |
| Total,........ | 55·1 | 54·0 | 53·8 | 52·4 | 51·5 | 50·2 | 49·4 | 48·4 | 47·5 | 46·7 |

There are also twenty-nine "model" schools in different parts of Ireland. These schools are managed directly by the Board of National Education, through their subordinates, and are usually supposed to be more efficient than the ordinary national schools. The school accommodation is much better, and the schoolmasters and schoolmistresses are of the highest grade, well qualified teachers naturally being chosen for these schools. The model schools in Dublin are very superior, and a critical visitor would see little to find fault with. The same might be said of the model schools in the provinces. It seems much to be desired that there should be more of these schools in all centres of population, however small. It need scarcely be remarked that they are "mixed"—*i.e.*, attended by children of all religious denominations, and that they, to quote the Commissioners' Report, "continue to maintain their high character." Many parents in the provinces send their children great distances every day to these schools, so high is their reputation. Though some people in Ireland are alive to the benefits to be derived from good education, as may be seen from the returns of attendance at the model schools,[1] yet there are others who are not, and, incredible as it may seem, there are persons to be found who object to these schools—why, it would be difficult to say.

Formerly all national school teachers were trained together at the training colleges in Marlborough Street, Dublin. In these, teachers belonging to different forms of religion were taught and trained side by side. This system had a liberalising effect more or less. But in 1883-4 separate denominational colleges were endowed. Grants were made to these for the first five years of their operation, amounting to three-fourths of their certified expenditure up to £50 a-year for masters, and £35 a-year for mistresses. At the end of this period grants were made on the credit system—*i.e.*, grants of £50 were made for male teachers, untrained, for one year, and of £100, if trained, for two years, and of £35 and £70 respectively for female teachers. These teachers should have passed through their college course, and afterwards have acted as teachers for a probationary term of two years. The teachers having at the end of that time obtained diplomas of training and competency to conduct schools, the colleges were credited with the above-named sums. In the Marlborough Street un-denominational training schools the system was different. In their case the entire cost was borne by the Commissioners of National Education out of the public purse. To abolish this inequality it was proposed, at the end of 1890, to make certain changes.

[1] Total number of pupils on rolls of model schools, who made any attendance for year 1890, was 14,235.

These were (1) to give a fixed grant in *all* colleges
(Marlborough Street included) of £50 a-year for males,
and of £35 a-year for females ; (2) to give, in addition,
a diploma bonus for males of £10, and of £7 for females
for each year of training on the award of the diploma
for training after a probationary service of two years
in the actual work of teaching.  The buildings of the
denominational colleges were also to be substantially
given to them on certain terms, so as to make them
in every way equal with the Marlborough Street
Training College.  These proposals were sanctioned
by the Commissioners of National Education, and are
now law.  The effect has been that the denominational
colleges and the Marlborough Street Training College
are now on an equal footing for all practical purposes.

There is a tendency on the part of students in
training at the Marlborough Street College to become
fewer in numbers, whilst the number of students
in training at the denominational colleges becomes
greater.  These respective decreases and increases
are likely to become more marked under the
changed conditions of the training colleges.  In the
subjoined table the actual figures for the past few
years may be compared :

## STUDENTS IN TRAINING.

| MARLBOROUGH STREET. | | DENOMINATIONAL COLLEGES. |
|---|---|---|
| 1886-7 | 200 | 288 |
| 1887-8 | 199 | 298 |
| 1888 9 | 200 | 293 |
| 1889-90 | 194 | 305 |

From these figures it will be seen not only that the number of students in denominational training colleges becomes greater, but also that more students are trained in these institutions than in the unsectarian Marlborough Street College.

From all these facts it will be seen (1) that mixed schools, that is, those in which children of all forms of religion are educated together, get proportionately fewer every year; (2) that from time to time great changes have been made in the system of training colleges. So much so, that now, instead of all national school teachers being trained together in one unsectarian college, the greater number are trained in denominational colleges; to this may be added the fact that, in the application grants for new schools in the year 1890, out of 144 managers all but 11 were clerics. This proportion is greater even than that in the already existing schools. These circumstances tend to make education in Ireland more and more sectarian every year. It is yet further demanded that schools which can show an attendance of one denomination only for three years shall be recognised as sectarian schools. The Presbyterian is the only body in Ireland which seems to be hostile to this continued movement in the direction of making education in Ireland more sectarian. Presbyterian teachers are usually educated at Marlborough Street Training College, and some prominent Presbyterians have loudly protested against levelling down that institution. The Presbyterian parts of Ireland being those in which the people are usually the best educated, members of that body may be looked on as favouring the best systems of training and teaching.

Ireland is one of the few parts of the British Isles in which there seems to be little desire for a good system of elementary education. Irishmen abroad are often said to be "hewers of wood and drawers of water" for the most part. If this is so, may not the fact be largely, if not wholly, due to want of education.

This is a brief account of the Irish system of education, compiled from the best sources.[1] Its actual working may be looked on from two points of view, first, as to the benefits it confers on the people ; and next, as to how far education is a check on crime.

There can be no doubt as to the great sharpness and intelligence of the little Irish boy or girl. As a traveller on foot in humble guise, I have often chatted with a barefooted urchin, who, going in the same direction, trotted by my side. These children were often entertaining companions, and could give a surprising amount of information as to the neighbouring country, together with shrewd, quaint comments on sundry personages. But, on inquiry, it might often be found that the child's book learning was by no means on a level with its natural intelligence. Sometimes the child did not attend school regularly, and often he did not go to school at all. According to the report of the Commissioners of National Education for 1890, the "percentage of average attendance to the average number of children on the rolls of the schools was but 59·0," and the percentage of school

[1] Reports issued by Commissioners of National Education, evidence of managers of schools, etc.

attendance to the estimated population of school age in Ireland would be less than 50.

Different reasons might be given for this small percentage of attendance. The chief reasons are, first, attendance at school not being compulsory, and next, education not being free. Irish parents, for the most part, do not value education so highly as they ought. And besides this, the children are useful for sundry small jobs, such as watching a cow that grazes on the roadside, running messages, and last, not least, minding other children who are smaller than themselves. If it has been found needful in England to legally enforce attendance at school, it is not to be wondered at that the same necessity should arise in Ireland.

The pence paid for school fees in Ireland may seem, to many people, a small matter. But in a country like Ireland, where little money circulates, and a number of the people are very poor, school pence are often not easily found every week. In 1890, £104,550 4s. 8d. was paid in school fees, being an average of 4s. 3¾d. per unit of average attendance. A sum like this could easily be found, either from the rates or the public purse, and one excuse at least for non-attendance would be taken away.

Want of clothes might often be pleaded as an excuse for non-attendance, but want of shoes hardly could, as it is the custom for many children, both in Scotland and Ireland, to go with bare feet. Many children, whose parents could well afford to buy them shoes, are barefooted, and the custom has much to recommend it, especially in a country like Ireland where there is little frost. The want of clothes is a more serious matter, particularly in wet weather and where the children have a long way to walk to school.

School accommodation in Ireland is often very bad and seldom good. There are different reasons for this state of things. One is that where a number of persons, or one person, builds a school, if the attendance falls below thirty, the school may be closed and become useless. Even though a grant may have been given by the Board of Commissioners, the local people have something to pay, and do not like to have their money thrown away. The result is, that, especially in thinly-peopled districts, the schools are small and the accommodation bad. I have often been struck, while walking through the country, with the poor, mean look of many of the schools, especially of those built by individuals.

Another reason for bad school accommodation is the desire on the part of each religious body to get a grant for its own school. In a small country town or village of about two thousand inhabitants are, or were, three national schools, none of them good ones. Two of these were attached to, and adjoined places of worship, one was "run" by a private individual with peculiar notions on religious matters. It was the opinion of all the best-informed townsmen, even of one of the clerics, that one good common school, managed by a committee, would be better for the town. All were agreed that the existing school buildings were small and unhealthy, and that the teachers might be better. It followed, as a matter of course, that one teaching staff, where there were now three, would be better paid from results and fees, and that, therefore, more highly-qualified teachers would seek to be employed. However, it proved impossible to bring about a reform. The "churches" stood in the way, also the "private person." They all preferred "unmixed" schools, and seemed to think that their children would be defiled by sitting side by side with those of other forms of religion.

Outbreaks both of pestilence and religious intolerance were common in this town; how far these might be traced to unhealthy school accommodation and to sectarian teaching it would not be difficult to say.

In another instance there was a good "mixed" school in a country district; the building stood apart from any place of worship, and had been built for children of different forms of religion. The "mixed" system did not please the members of one or more of the denominations in the neighbourhood. Accordingly a new school was built, and a number of children withdrawn from the old one. This was done in face of the fact that the gross population of the district was diminishing, from emigration and other causes. The consequence was, that the teachers of the old school became worse off from the falling away of "results" and fees, and the teachers of the new school would be poorly paid because of the fewness of their pupils. The managers of the schools would thus be unable to get good teachers, and the cause of education would suffer thereby. If the returns as to the falling off in the number of mixed schools are to be trusted (as there is no doubt they are),[1] this is but one instance out of many.

[1] Report of Commissioners of National Education.

I

Education may also be looked on as to its relation to crime. This relation is twofold, first to the bloodshed caused by party riots, and next to that caused by agrarian outrages. These are the two most serious forms of crime in Ireland, and education, or the want of it, has to do with both.

Although, as has been already stated, race has more to do with party riots than religion, still, the latter enters into the matter more or less. Especially when it is remembered that a historical and political flavour is imparted to much Irish religious teaching. Now, it is greatly to be regretted that sectarian teaching of this sort is gaining ground in Ireland. If there is one country in Europe in which there exists the greatest need for teaching children of different religions in the same school, it is Ireland. Yet it is found from the reports of the Commissioners of National Education that "mixed" schools get fewer every year. In those cases which have come under my notice, I have always found in "mixed" districts, that where the schools are also "mixed," there is less religious animosity. The reasons for this must be quite plain : the children belonging to differing forms of religion sit side by side, and get to know and love one another. Besides this, friendships are formed in early life which ripen and continue into middle and old age. Under these circumstances, people are much less likely to quarrel with each other. Where the schools are sectarian or unmixed, the children know nothing of each other, and form often quite wrong notions as to what those of a different religion may be like.

When party riots form such serious difficulties in

managing Ireland, it might be thought that everything would be done to soften these animosities; and
that instead of making education more sectarian, it
would have been made less so. It is generally supposed that the best way of making people friends
with each other is to bring them together. It is also
a common notion that friendships are formed often in
early life, and many people will stint themselves so
as to be able to send their children to costly schools
where they may make fine friends. People in Ireland do not seem to share these notions, they appear to
think that the cause of harmony and friendship is
best promoted by separating children into hostile
camps.

The want of education has much to do with crime
and outrage. If the statistics of crime and those of
ignorance are carefully studied, it will be found that
the most ignorant counties in Ireland are also the
most criminal. In Galway, Kerry, or Clare, the proportion of the inhabitants who can read and write is
very small—among the smallest in Ireland. And from
the returns of crime for the year 1890, these were the
three most criminal counties in Ireland.[1] On the
other hand, in the counties of Wicklow and Down,
where most of the inhabitants are able to read and
write, it will be found that the proportion of crimes
and outrages is very small. In fact, these two counties will compare favourably with any part of the
British Isles so far as crime is concerned.

This freedom from crime must, to a great extent, be accounted for by the people being com-

---

[1] Parliamentary return of offences in Ireland for 1890.

paratively well educated. Wicklow is, for the most part, a very Celtic county, and Down, on the other hand, is chiefly lowland Scotch with Norman Irish and Celtic districts, so that race has not much to do with the matter. Neither has religion; for in different parts of the county of Down different forms of religion are professed, yet all are peaceful. The same may be said to a lesser degree of Wicklow. Other counties might also be quoted in support of this view, but these two have appeared to be the most suitable. It will be found, almost without exception, that, in those parts of Ireland having a high educational record, there is but little crime. It will be found in Ireland, as elsewhere, that ignorance and crime go hand in hand.

The subject of higher education scarcely comes within the province of these pages. It has little to do with the common social life of Ireland, and is a subject with which most readers of newspapers are familiar.

# CONCLUSION.

SUCH matters as are of greatest moment to Ireland having been treated of, there are a few circumstances of minor interest which may deserve a passing notice. These are chiefly of a social nature and are peculiar to those in different ranks of life, but they all bear more or less directly on weighty questions.

The first of these social aspects of Irish life which may be noticed is the remarkable chastity of the people. And this is all the more noticeable, because Irish marriages are very seldom what may be termed "love matches." This is to be most plainly seen among the peasantry of all parts of Ireland. Indeed, it is one of many respects in which Ireland resembles France. Most Irish peasant maids have dowries, however small; these "fortunes" range from a feather-bed or a goose or a few ducks up to several hundred pounds. The dowry is everything to the suitor, who on his part is expected to be able to keep a wife in the "condition to which she has been accustomed." As this "condition" varies, so must that of the expectant bridegroom. A "poor man" must not look for the hand of a rich peasant's daughter, nor must a man of the working-class or a farm servant dare to cast his eyes on a farmer's daughter. Young men and women sometimes marry out of their rank in life, but it is looked on as something "dreadful." I remember once telling a young man that he ought to pay his addresses to the daughter of a neighbouring farmer. The youth's reply was that " the dog would be set on him if he went near the house." This young man's father farmed about twenty acres and the lady's father farmed about sixty acres.

Notwithstanding all this bargaining and buying and selling, there is comparatively little illegitimacy in Ireland. The percentage of illegitimate births in European countries is given as 2·6 in Ireland, 4·9 in England, 8·5 in Scotland, 7·92 in France, 8·1 in Belgium, 9·29 in Germany, 14·5 in Austria.[1] From these figures Ireland is found to compare favourably with the principal countries in Europe.

The upper classes in, or of, Ireland seem to be greatly out of sympathy with the people, although formerly it was quite otherwise. This may be explained from the fact that at one time the better classes were brought up more in Ireland and understood the people better. Popular movements of the olden time never wanted a scion of some of the great families to head them. Popular leaders of the present day are made of entirely different stuff. The great landowners of Ireland are Englishmen to all intents and purposes. They are often not even born in Ireland, and men, bearing Irish names and titles, have little else about them that is Irish. They are brought up in England and know little or nothing of Ireland or its needs. The social strata underlying this last-named are also greatly anglicised, but in this instance it is a veneer or varnish, and, perhaps, for that reason

[1] In 1885.

they are more unpopular. Many of the smaller land-owners, agents, and persons of the official classes belong to this strata. Another reason for the unpopularity of people of this class is, that circumstances compel them to live in Ireland, and hence they come more into collision with the people than the aristocracy do.

Of late years it has become the fashion with people who can afford it to send their sons and daughters to English schools. Whatever they may gain is more than counterbalanced by their learning habits and manners that are quite unsuited to Ireland, where the conditions of life are different from those in England. That "ancient and illustrious University,"[1] Trinity College, Dublin, is now quite discredited among the Irish "classes," why, it would be difficult to say, as its graduates are distinguished both in the learned professions and in the public service.[2] Even professors and fellows of Trinity College send their sons to English colleges, although in some cases it must severely tax their narrow means to do so. I have also known of second-rate Dublin and provincial lawyers sending their sons to Eton and other English public schools. At these places they learn things and acquire habits which quite unfit them for the lives they have to lead in their own country. Notwithstanding this, it is thought to be the "right thing" for young Irish men and women to have their brogues electro-plated with English accents.

[1] Late Professor Fawcett.

[2] A long list might be made of great Trinity College graduates. Sir C. Russell among the living, and the late Archbishop of York among those lately deceased, may be mentioned.

The results of this policy are somewhat remarkable. To begin with, the middle-class is rent in twain, one strata being Englified, the other not. Of course, the former despises the latter, and this breeds ill-will and want of confidence. And, furthermore, it causes many people to dislike England, who would not otherwise do so. English breeding does not always produce loyalty to England or its Queen. Some of the most disloyal Irishmen have been educated in England, and, on the other hand, I have never met with better or more loyal subjects than some home-bred Irish people. It is much to be regretted that the present system of educating the " better classes " does not tend to increase their number. Its tendency has been more and more to cause divisions, even among people of the same class. There is a growing tendency on the part of the Anglo-Irish to become in Ireland, what the English colonies are on the continent of Europe. On the other hand, the bulk of the people draw more and more away from the " classes," and come under the guidance of men whose whole feeling is anti-British.

As is well known, the aristocracy of Ireland turn their backs to that country. Sometimes they visit it for a little time, but that is all. A resident nobleman is a rare thing. In the capital there are now no noblemen's town houses—the last was " put down " some years ago. As a consequence, society is a mixture of that of an English garrison town and of a Crown colony. The chief personages in the capital are the judges and higher officials, next come the professional men and merchants, after these the general public. There is also a large garrison.

There is neither an aristocracy of birth nor of intellect. Of late years some rich parvenus have sprung up in Dublin, whence or how no one knows but themselves. These people entertain lavishly, and form a circle of their own in addition to the Castle society. Not but that they likewise go to Court. Levee and drawing-room are open to all persons introduced by those who have been previously admitted themselves. Introductions are easily to be had. No commonly well-conducted person who can buy, borrow, or get on credit the needful dress, is refused. All this grandeur turns the heads of the Irish middle-class, and they give themselves airs that English people of the same rank in life would not think of putting on. The result is that lawyers, agents, and business men speak in haughty tones to the common folk with whom they have dealings. This "high and mightiness" is bitterly resented (always behind backs), and the keen wit of the Dublin lower class finds a vent in satirising those above them. Too often the latter are food for satire. It is not easy for people to ape the manners and habits of a different class without becoming absurd.

These offensive and ridiculous manners spread from the capital into the country districts, and have a great effect in rousing the ill-will of the peasant. No people, so far as I have seen, are so easily won by kindness as the Irish; they respond at once to any sympathy, provided it is genuine. But they are very sharp-witted, and quick to discern the true from the false. They are also resentful of any harsh or overbearing conduct. Having been long kept down, they do not always express this feeling, but nevertheless it rankles in their minds, and often bears bitter fruit in after years. Now, a man, English-bred, and having an unduly high opinion of his dignity, cannot well be otherwise than hateful to the Irish peasant. Even where willing to sympathise, he is unable to do so, because he does not understand the countryman's feelings. But the agent or official is generally thinking of how he can best impress the people with a sense of his greatness.

It is also a very fashionable thing to look on the people as though they were some uncivilised race, to be patronised by those above them. This sentiment is even to be found in the north of Ireland, where all classes are of the same race. I have heard parvenus in that province speak of people, to whom possibly they were related, as the " aborigines."

All this is very silly and absurd, and anywhere but in Ireland would be beneath notice. But Ireland is peculiarly circumstanced, and the Irish are a sensitive and resentful people, hence this pretence and affectation do incalculable mischief. The upper classes and the mass of the people in Ireland are now very much strangers and foreigners to each other. And nothing can be worse for the country than such a state of things.

The common notion that the Irish people are sentimental and humorous is a mistaken one on the whole. What the Irish may have been in former days it is not easy to know. If the droll tales published half a century ago were true of those times, they are certainly not true of these. But it may be doubted if these popular Irish stories were ever otherwise than gross exaggerations. They have done—one of them in particular[1]—a vast amount of harm in giving English people a wholly false notion of the Irish character. Every one who visits Ireland, or writes anything about that country, seems to think themselves bound to discover, and make public, something absurd or sentimental. The Irishman is expected to be either a ruffian or a buffoon, or a picturesque martyr; anything, in fact, but a commonplace, quiet subject of the English crown, what the great majority of the Irish people are. Unhappily, there is, as has been already shown, a limited area of disturbance in Ireland. Of late years this has been a happy hunting-ground for correspondents of newspapers, sensation-mongers, and " carpet-baggers of all sorts." Everything in this part of Ireland has been so fully described and made the most of in every way that it is needless to do more than refer to the subject here. " Martyrdom " and " ruffianism " have each been found here, according to the point of view of the correspondent or " tripper." But humour seems to have been wanting for the most part. Were a person of an inquiring disposition to make a tour all over Ireland, travelling slowly, and minutely inquiring into everything, he would find these " popular " Irish qualities absent almost altogether.

I remember once meeting at a little watering-place, in a very Irish part of Ireland, three English tourists. They had come to Ireland full of notions about the " absurd funny " Irishman, and were anxious to see and talk with him. For this purpose they hired a car

[1] " Handy Andy."

for a drive through a wild mountainous district, where they spent the day visiting among the inhabitants. In the evening they returned, disgusted at their want of success in their search for native wit and humour. Still, at the principal tourist resorts, a supply of buffoonery and sham sentiment may be found, in order to suit the English demand. It is quite a business this sort of acting, and the dress, jokes, and stories are all carefully studied beforehand. Nor, indeed, are stage effects of this sort confined to Ireland. Every one who has travelled much knows the picturesque peasants, who, during the season, are got up in national costumes, and who, out of the season, are dressed like the rest of the people.

The poorer classes of people in the city of Dublin are the only people in Ireland, as a class, who display any powers of humour or satire. In Dublin, Irish wit yet lingers, but there is said to be a much smaller supply than was formerly the case. Still, the tourist travelling in search of Irish humour, may not find the Dublin "jarvey" altogether disappointing.

Irish "beggars" have long been a reproach to the sister isle. Few things must be more painful to a spirited Irishman in England or abroad than to have this reproach of "beggary" cast in his teeth. Especially when it is borne in mind that Irishmen, whether in England or the Colonies, are among the most hardworking members of the community. Whether as professional men, or labourers in docks, shipyards, or ironworks, Irishmen are among the most useful people in England and could be ill spared. Poor though the "harvestman" is, he is rarely a "cadger," and many an English harvest would rot on the ground but for his active and willing hands. Yet, notwithstanding all this, there are good grounds for the reproach of "Irish beggar." It is a settled policy on the part of Irishmen of different classes to make the worst of everything Irish. Not being in their secrets, I cannot pretend to know the reasons for this habit of displaying, and making the most of, Irish rags and sores. But it may be supposed that it is in order to excite pity, and as a consequence to get something that could not otherwise be had. As it is from England that this something is to be had, it seems to be quite lost sight of that many Englishmen "dislike giving to beggars." Why poverty should be a qualification in order to receive increased political concessions it would not be easy to imagine. Some people might think that an appearance of independence and thrift would be the very reason why a country should possess greater powers of self-government.

The "beggar" principle is carried out sometimes to an extent that should make an honest Irishman blush with shame. If Irishmen at home knew the amount of harm done abroad by this practice of making the worst of everything, they would soon put it down. The worst result, perhaps, is, that when partial famines or seasons of real distress occur, it becomes difficult to get English aid. The reply usually is, " Oh, the Irish are always begging." This remark is untrue of the bulk of the Irish people, but, unhappily, is true of many public persons, and of the cadgers who swarm about tourist resorts. It is from these classes that most English people get their ideas of what Irishmen are like.

Not long since in the neighbourhood of a tourist resort was a miserable-looking cabin. It was not far from the side of a road, along which ran a public conveyance every day. Whenever the vehicle passed, a child clad in one scanty ragged garment came out of the cabin and ran along by the side of the car. He first ran by one side looking with mute, piteous gaze on the passengers seated thereon. He then ran by the other side and repeated the performance. The child said nothing, but the "get up" and the "glance" were both very touching. He always got alms, as he was a most pitiful-looking object. After a time some inquiries were made as to how there could be people in such want in the locality. It was then discovered that the child's cabin was that of a small farmer who was a tenant of a rich parvenu landlord. The tenant was poor enough, but no worse off than his neighbours on the same property who did not beg. In this way a great injury was done to the deserving poor. Of course, the landlord indirectly encouraged the idea of begging by allowing the cabin to be in such a miserable state. Here, side by side, were two of the worst features of modern Irish life, the pauper in the tenant, and the coarse parvenu in the landlord.

Among the Irish peasantry generally there is very little mendicancy, and many of them in bad seasons endure great privation uncomplainingly. Irish begging is almost altogether professional. There is the beggar with a large wallet, usually an old man or woman, who have their "rounds," and receive alms in kind—*i.e.,* scraps and potatoes. These people rarely beg from the passer-by, and generally supply their patrons with news in return for food and shelter. They are usually a harmless class of people, and are quiet and well-conducted in their own way. There are also the beggars and cadgers of the tourist resorts. These are quite too well known to need any description. It may be enough to state that they are often great humbugs and liars, but their profits are not large, the tourist season being a short one. There are also other people who may be termed beggars, though they would be very wrathful if told so. I mean those persons in different ranks of life who point out the worst of everything in Ireland, and are always telling Englishmen how poor everyone and everything is. This is only one side of the matter. Although there is much poverty in Ireland there is also much wealth—far more than is generally supposed. As a rule it is very unequally distributed, and money does not circulate as it should. In the north of Ireland the poorer classes are better off than those in or near the metropolis, simply because money circulates. But in Ulster there is little realised wealth. There is a show of business, and much business is done. But a large concern, which employs one or two thousand persons, often pays little or no interest to its proprietors. And at the present time it would be difficult to realise most kinds of business property in Ulster. In and around Dublin and Meath the case is just the reverse—there is much realised wealth, but little circulation of it. Brewing, grazing, cattle shipping are paying businesses, but give little employment.

And much money is hoarded and not employed in
any way.

The Northerns certainly cannot be accused of "beggary." Their policy is just the reverse. They always
exaggerate anything they have, and boast of being
the richest part of Ireland. In this, the general
opinion is, that they are wrong. They do more business than people elsewhere in Ireland, but, as a rule,
they are not "worth much." But in some parts of
the North the professional beggar may be found
making the worst of everything.

It must not be supposed that people who expose
rags and sores to certain other persons in order to
suit their own purposes are always acting on this
principle. By no means; few people are so purse-
proud, and measure everything so much by a money
standard as the Irish "classes." There are several
reasons for this state of things. In the first place,
people in Ireland have usually either nothing or a
very great deal. That is to say, there are professional
men, clerks in public and private employ, men with
situations of different kinds, and a host of poor peasants
and labourers, all of whom have just what they can
earn. Few of these classes can be said to "have
anything." On the other hand are rich graziers,
cattle salesmen, brewers, distillers, publicans, provision
merchants, and others. These are usually men, rich
according to their rank in life, and many of them are
considerable landowners. They form in fact the aristocracy of Ireland. They are the propertied classes,
and some of them would be rich men anywhere.
Publicans and shopkeepers in Dublin and Drogheda

have died worth one or two hundred thousand pounds. And others, such as brewers and distillers, have much more than these sums. There being no real aristocracy living in Ireland, and the aristocracy of talent, whether professional or literary, finding its best market in England, it follows that the parvenu has it all his own way. Most people yield to them in private life, and the distinction of persons "according to what they have got" is carried into all classes, from the large landowner to the well-off peasant. As already stated, society in Dublin consists chiefly of the official and professional classes, with some parvenus as well. But, as a rule, the latter are either too coarse and plain, or too grand for Dublin society. The one variety finds its pleasures at home, and the other disports itself abroad or in London.

If anyone cared to take the trouble of inquiring into the pecuniary resources of Ireland he would be surprised to find how rich a country it was in many ways, although side by side with all this wealth, both in money and in kind, is a fearful amount of squalor and poverty. There are many people able to do much to remedy this, but who will not do so. The Irish parvenu is at the same time profuse and mean. He is fond of display, and will often lavishly entertain any great or distinguished Englishman. At the same time people on his estate may live in wretched cabins, or people in his employment may be ground down to starvation wages. He will bully people who are in any way dependent on him, and drive the hardest bargains with those who are needy. This policy does not tend to make the country or its in-

K

habitants more prosperous-looking, hence travellers form bad impressions of it.

Except in the North, there is not generally in Ireland any of that dislike on the part of the masses against those who are better off than themselves, simply because they are so. Display and stylishness are admired rather than otherwise. The salary of the Dublin Lord-Mayor has been trebled by popular consent in order that he may keep up a greater show and state. The people dislike the rich, especially the parvenus, because of their stinginess and illiberality in small matters, not because of any display on their part. The complaint is that they do not spend enough among the people, and seek so many of their pleasures in other lands, often returning to Ireland in order to economise. The agents and officials through the country have little, spend less, and are usually haughty and disagreeable in their manners, hence they are doubly hateful in the eyes of the people. A popular man in Ireland is one that spends money freely among the people, gives liberally in charity, and is pleasant and affable to everyone. Even one whose means are limited, but who does his best in these respects, is as much beloved by the masses as one whose means are much greater, and who spends more.

---

In the preceding pages an honest effort has been made to set down the results of many years' experience and careful inquiry. There has been no attempt made to write up or write down any particular view of Irish affairs. Everything has been described as it appeared to the observer. The sentiments of the people have been recorded, but nothing more. Whether their opinions are right or wrong, it is not for the writer of this book to state. The great importance of the subject must form the only excuse for writing these pages at all. Many of them must have seemed tiresome to the reader, but it is difficult to write of a commonplace peasant life without the account seeming dull at times. Much might have been done to enliven these pages by anecdotes, but it has seemed to the writer that Irish anecdotes have been overdone. They are quite well, rather too well, known, and, on the other hand, the common social life and condition of the country are but little known. To describe these faithfully and truthfully has been the object of the writer.[1]

[1] See appendix M.

THE END.

*Printed by Cowan & Co., Limited, Perth.*

# APPENDIX.

(A, Page 7.)

WHAT has been stated here may seem absurd to some persons, nevertheless it describes a state of things which really exists. The editor knew of another case where a young man inheriting property was gravely told that he could not possibly be looked upon as a "gentleman" unless he had at least "four thousand a-year." In this case, as in that in the first chapter, the object of the remark was a man of ancient family, blameless character, and independent means. This state of things, no doubt, does not exist in every part of Ireland : in some few places there are very "small," and very poor gentry, but in most rural districts the "gentry" consist of agents who are supposed to stand in their employer's shoes, *pro tem*, landowners, who, though nearly always "hard up," yet have large houses and extensive properties, and parvenus, of one sort or another, generally connected with "whisky" or "grazing," these latter being usually rich men.

A state of society such as this may be found in counties where the bulk of the people are very poor. A resident gentry, in the common sense of the term, is greatly needed in Ireland.

M'Whirter here expresses the sentiments of most Irish Conservatives, especially those in Ulster. Conservatism in Ireland is quite different from Conservatism anywhere else. Owing to a curious complication of matters in the past which need not here be gone into, a class of people in Ireland are Conservative on one or two points, and not so on anything else. It was at one time the policy of the Tories to (very inconsistently) back up Irish Protestants who were Radicals to the backbone. Hence their support was gained, and has been kept down to the present, though whether the Conservative party may be able to keep it

149

in the future is very doubtful. Political Protestantism is the test, almost the only one, of a "sound Conservative" in Ireland. Conservatism has been much less of a class question than in England, many, if not most, of the great Irish landowners having always been Liberals.[1] In a great number of cases within the editor's personal knowledge, Irish Conservatives, especially those of the middle-class, have become Liberals on going to live in England.

Their Puritan origin, and the fact of so many, if not most, Irish Protestants being Nonconformists, may account to some extent for this fact.

### (B, Page 11, Bogs.)

As most English readers may not be familiar with Irish bogs, a short account of them may be of interest.

Irish bogs are of different kinds, varying from a "wet spot" between two little hills to a vast plain of peat and heather. The common bogs or moist places are much like those to be found in Devonshire and elsewhere in England, and require little or no description save that Irish bogs of this kind usually contain more peat than those in England.

The great bogs of Ireland correspond in some respects to the "fen districts" of England, but in other ways are very different. The bogs resemble the fens in that they are perfectly level, contain peat, and often adjoin marshes. There is also in both cases a distinction between "bog" and "marsh," as there is a difference between "marsh land and fen land." Here the likenesses end, and the unlikenesses begin. In the first place, a bog is unlike a fen in that it contains much more peat suitable for fuel. Peat stacks may no doubt be found in the fen districts, but they are not on the whole common, and the peats are difficult to get. Peat fuel abounds in the Irish bogs, and is to be

---

[1] If the lists of landowners are studied, it will be found that the Lansdowne, Kenmare, Devonshire, Clanricarde, Leinster, Fitzwilliam, and many other great families have been Liberals.

had everywhere, the reason for this being, that the peat in the Irish bog is less mixed with other matters than that of the fens. However, if there is a gain in fuel, there is a very great loss in other respects, because fen is capable of reclamation, being mixed with other substances, and Irish bog is, on the whole, incapable of reclamation. Small patches of bog have been reclaimed by bringing clay from a distance and mixing it with the peat. This has been done with some of the small Ulster bogs lying between little hills, but the process seemed a troublesome one, and the reclaimed bog was only suitable for roots or meadow. These are the only instances of reclaimed bog which the editor has seen. The great bogs seem to be quite incapable of being reclaimed on any wide scale for the reason before stated.

An Irish bog is much drier than an English fen, and for this reason a dry spot in or near a bog is much healthier than an "isle" in the fens. No mist or miasma rises from a bog where "marsh" is absent, hence people living on the borders of large bogs are often very healthy and free from ague, which is more than can be said for the inhabitants of many of the fens. Another result of this peculiar dryness of the bogs is, that heather grows to a great height on many of them, and grouse thrive apace where they are preserved. In fact many of the large Irish bogs may be described as moors flattened out, being often quite as dry as the latter, and sometimes easier to walk over. The great "banks," as they are called, of dry peat are very remarkable; these are often many feet, or as it is called "spits," in depth, a "spit" being the length of a peat or "sod of turf."

Few or no Irish counties are without more or less of bogs, but in the eastern and north-eastern counties, they are very small and far between; besides this, most of them have been "cut away." "Cut-away bog," or "spent moss," as it is called in parts of Ulster, means bog from which all the peat has been cut It forms a very ugly object, full of holes of black, slimy water, and beds of gravel or stone which underlie the peat. In castern Ireland coal is cheaper than in the south of England, the collieries of Lancashire and Cumberland not being far off, and sea carriage being cheaper than that by rail. It is well for the people of these parts of Ireland that coal is reasonable in price, as there are few woods or bogs whence fuel could be obtained. The peat bogs of Ireland are chiefly in the central parts of the country, hence those districts lying between them and the east coast are worst off for fuel, coal being dear, and "turf" scarce or altogether absent. These great central bogs of Ireland contain a practically exhaustless supply of peat fuel. Much of this is brought to Dublin by barges, and great stacks of peat or "turf" are to be seen on the canal banks near the bridges. Two canals lead from Dublin to the Shannon, the chief traffic on these being turf or produce from the rural districts, and coal and timber from Dublin. It is a curious fact that coal, chiefly for public institutions, such as barracks and workhouses in the central parts of Ireland, is brought by canal from Dublin. It is said that it is more economical than peat, though the latter abounds in these localities. Some people in the country also think it "vulgar" to burn "turf;" besides this, modern grates are not suited for burning it. But "turf" is the fuel of the peasantry, wherever they can get it. They cut it themselves usually, so that it costs merely the small payments made to the landowner for the "turf bank." These bog rents are often very nominal, besides this, most farms in boggy counties have what is called "turbarry," or right of cutting turf attached. Peat is burned on an open fireplace of the old fashion, the sods or peats being built in little heaps. In Dublin, "turf" is quite too costly for burning alone, it is only used to help to burn bad coal used by the poor, or for lighting fires. "Turf-cutting" affords employment to many persons in the central parts of Ireland, and there are villages chiefly inhabited by "turf-cutters." Some years ago, experiments were made with machinery to make a hard, durable peat fuel ; this was brought to Dublin in small circular discs, but, for some reason or other, the manufacture was given up. Lately, a company has been formed for the purpose of making "peat fuel," with what success remains yet to be seen.

These bogs take up a great space. The largest, called "the bog of Allan," extends over several counties, not in one unbroken tract, but winding in and out. In some places, it is so broad that it bounds the horizon, a sea of peat and heather lying in front of the spectator.

Peat has a power of preserving things covered therewith for a great length of time. Many objects of interest have been discovered in the Irish bogs in a wonderfully good state of preservation, notably the remains of the Irish elk, a gigantic animal for centuries extinct.

In the Dublin museums, many objects of interest may be seen which have been discovered in Irish peat bogs.

In most parts of Ireland, peat bogs are called "bogs," and peats are called "sods of turf," nor, if other names were used, would the people understand what was meant. In parts of Ulster, bogs are called "mosses," and peats are called "peats."

### (C, Page 16, Protection.)

Protectionist ideas seem to the editor to be gaining ground greatly in Ireland. There are many reasons for this feeling. Manufacture of cloth has been lately started on a more extensive scale, and people find that they are unable to keep pace with English manufacturers, having better machinery and more capital. Besides this, French and American notions are very popular in Ireland, and France and the United States are well known to be protectionist countries. It is not considered prudent to say much about protection at present, but there is little doubt that sooner or later a demand for it will arise. This demand will come chiefly from the working-class, many of whom are thrown out of employment by the cheapness of English goods. The Dublin working-class bitterly complain of the want of patriotism of their fellow-townsmen and women,

who buy English-made dress materials and shoes, simply because they are cheaper than those made at home.  Dublin was
at one time a great centre of the Irish boot and shoe trade,
these being made of excellent quality.  This industry has been
almost destroyed by the introduction of cheap English machine-
made boots and shoes.  Irish makers cannot possibly compete
with these, and the Irish public, screaming patriots included,
buy the English-made article simply because it is cheaper than
that made at home.  It is the same with dress of other kinds.
Poplin and tabinet are beautiful materials, at one time largely
manufactured in Dublin, but Irish ladies are not sufficiently
patriotic to wear them.  And stuffs of English or foreign manufacture are now worn at the drawing-rooms and vice-regal balls
instead of home-made fabrics.

Among the general public there is the same want, or alleged
want, of patriotism, in buying cheap English shoddies and stuffs,
partly because they are cheaper, and yet more, because they are
considered more fashionable and smarter than the old-fashioned
woollens and friezes.  It is, no doubt, a great proof of the
" union of hearts " between certain people in Ireland and others
in England, that the former should enrich the latter at the cost
of the semi-famished Irish working-class.

### (D, Page 23, Antiquities.)

The eastern part of Ireland, north of Dublin, is particularly
rich in the remains of abbeys and castles.  Some of these are of
great size and beauty.  King John's Castle at Trim, Bective
Abbey, Carlingford Abbey, the ruins of the Archiepiscopal
palace at Swords, near Dublin, and many other historic remains are in Leinster.  A little to the north in Lecale in Ulster,
are ruins of numerous castles along the coast.  There are few
parts of the British Isles where so many Norman castles can be
found close to each other.  Most Irish ruins, ecclesiastical or
civil, are greatly neglected, especially along the Ulster coast,
where no one seems to care for them.  The editor has known of

quantities of stones being taken from ruins of great interest to build cow-houses. Ruins in many instances are crumbling to the dust for want of a little care on the part of the lord of the soil.

### (E, Page 26.)

In old surveys large parts of the county Down may be seen, which had not in the middle of the seventeenth century been as yet mapped out into town lands. The divided or mapped-out country went a certain distance and then ceased : all beyond was apparently uninhabited "bush" or "prairie." These districts are now well peopled, and are thickly studded with farm-steads and fields.

### (F, Page 34, Names of Places.)

The English translation of a few of the chief Irish prefixes may be of interest. *Bally* is an Anglicised corruption of the Celtic *Bala*, a place. The Irish peasantry never pronounce the final y in this word. *Balla* in Ballachulish in Scotland is the same word. *Kil* means a church, or more strictly a cell, the ancient Irish churches having been very small. *Drum* means a long hill ; *Dun*, a small mound or earthwork ; *Lis*, a fort, usually of stakes ; *Rath*, also a fort ; *More* = great ; *Beg* = small ; *Bawn* = white ; *Dubh*, pronounced *duv* or *daff* = black ; *Lin* = a pool ; Dublin originally pronounced *Duvelin* = dark pool ; *Inver* = a river ; *Ben* = a peak ; *Slieve* = a mountain. Most of these words may also be found in the Scotch Highlands.

### (G, Page 60, Horses and Ponies.)

There is now much talk and correspondence about improving the horses and ponies in the far west of Ireland. Yorkshire hackney stallions have been already imported by the State, and several of these were lately "on view" in Dublin. Opinions on the matter have differed very widely. Some people have stated that these are the wrong sort of horses for the little western ponies and mares, and that Clydesdale sires would have been better. Others, with whom the editor is disposed to agree, are opposed to Clydesdale or any other form of "cart blood." The size of the progeny of Clydesdales and the little Irish mares is urged strongly as an argument in their favour, but this size is little use for ordinary harness purposes, if accompanied with sluggishness. Though English buyers may at first be taken in by the size and appearance of this cross, they will soon find out its bad qualities, and in the end the character of the Irish horse will suffer. There seems little doubt that the Yorkshire hackney stallions are much more likely to breed good harness horses of small size and low price than any sort of cart horse would be likely to do. The chief objection to the lately imported animals is, first, that their quality is not good enough, and next, that their number is not nearly large enough. They are certainly a better kind to breed with than either cart horses or weedy thoroughbreds. But in the editor's opinion it would be much better to keep these western ponies pure, and if stallions were imported, that they should be of the Highland pony family. It is a great pity that this Irish pony has been so much neglected of late years, and that males of the true Connemara breed are scarce. In this pure state these ponies are both more easily kept by the poor people on the west coast, and bring better prices in the open market, than cross-bred animals.

In the county of Antrim the native ponies have been greatly spoiled by the introduction of Suffolk blood. The result of the cross is a chestnut or black cobby animal, in no respect, save size, so good as the original pony.

### (H, Page 73.)

Magistrates here mean unpaid or county magistrates. As nearly everyone knows, there are a great number of stipendiary resident magistrates in Ireland; these men have nothing to do with fiscal or poor law business. Loud complaints have been made through the Irish parliamentary representatives as to this latter class of magistrate. Their inferiority and excessive number seem to be the chief grounds of objection. As to the first charge, there seems no reason why paid magistrates should not be barristers of certain standing as in England. As to the second objection, though it would be impossible to do without paid magistrates in some places, yet the present number might be reduced, and in quiet counties such officials might be dispensed with. To a certain extent this has been already done, as in some instances there is but one stipendiary for an entire county.

(I, Page 89, Protestant Rebels.)

At the close of the last century most Ulster Protestants were in a state of open rebellion. Some hotly contested battles took place between the insurgents and the King's troops, in which the former were defeated with some difficulty. At this time the Protestants were to some extent divided in opinion, a considerable minority being loyal to England. Should all join together in rebellion at any time the results might be serious, and this is a danger which must always be reckoned with.

(J, Page 95, Land Courts.)

As is well known, Irish rents are now fixed by a court of land commissioners for a term of fifteen years. This system of fixing rents has not, on the whole, given much satisfaction, especially to the smaller landholders. To understand some of the reasons for this want of confidence, a short account of Irish land valuation becomes needful.

The whole of Ireland was valued many years ago by a number of official valuers. This valuation was called "Griffith's valuation," and was commonly supposed to be one-fourth under the actual letting value of land at the time before the present agricultural depression began. Even at this time "Griffith" was not considered to represent the true value of the land. The valuation had been made at a time when wheat was dear and labour cheap, and when cattle and sheep commanded much smaller prices than at present. The impression a few years ago was that the strong corn-growing land, especially that in the eastern parts of Ireland, was too highly valued, and on the other hand, that pasture and light turnip-growing land was quite too cheaply valued. From the alteration in the respective values of corn and stock, it was quite to be expected that land should also alter as to its valuation. Another proof of these changed values was to be found in the prices bid for interests in farms. In many cases " Griffith " was no guide whatever. Some land let at or near this valuation was thought to be too dear, other land let much above Griffith was considered cheap. Matters stood thus when the present land courts were established. One of the first grounds of discontent with these courts was, that their powers were at once too limited and too full. They were said to be too limited because leaseholds and grazing-farms did not come within the scope of their operation. And, on the other hand, landlords complained because rents were fixed on farms which were practically grazing land. They also complained of rents being fixed on land which had been let for short terms, where the tenant had made no improvements, and was expected to give up the land after the expiration of the few years for which it had been let. Both landlords and tenants were also dissatisfied with the constitution of the land courts, some members of which were not considered to be competent authorities on the subject of land valuation. In one instance, a tailor and draper in a country town was appointed a land commissioner. He may have been fully qualified to value land, but the fact of his business being well-known was not one to give him weight with the agricultural interest.

In making their decisions, the courts were considered by the tenantry to have been too much guided by " Griffith," and to have valued some land too highly. This land, near the coast, was both valued highly and let at dear rents, and in former times was no doubt quite worth these rents for wheat-growing. But the drop in the rents was not thought to anything like correspond to the fall in the price of grain. This kind of land being ill-suited for grazing and the tenant having usually made all improvements, he found himself in a difficult position. He could not turn grazier, and if he threw up his farm he lost his property. On the other hand, many tenants who had good grazing land had their rent considerably lowered, often in cases where the reduction was not needed by the occupier.

At the subcommission courts held in the country districts, these land cases are fiercely fought out, lawyers being engaged by both landlord and tenant. Whatever abatement the tenant may get, he certainly pays for it in law costs. Nor does the matter end here, for appeals from the decisions of the sub-commissioners to the higher courts in Dublin are common, and this means yet greater expense.

Fixing rents in the "congested" districts in the south and west of Ireland is merely a ghastly kind of joke. These places are unfit for human habitation, and the people would be sunk in misery even did they pay no rent. As it is, their rents are trifling, often not more than two or three pounds annually, and this frequently in arrear for a length of time.

Public sentiment in Ireland may be said to be generally in favour of absolute ownership of the land by the occupier. Well considered schemes of land purchase, where the provisions of the enactments are simple and easily understood, will always be popular. The only remedy for the "congested" districts is to be found either in moving the people on to the uninhabited pastoral tracts or in some scheme of State-aided emigration.

### (K, Page 118.)

This may be a proper place to mention people who, though not labourers or peasants, yet on the whole belong to, or are drawn from, those classes.

Workers in factories are chiefly women belonging to the poorer class of peasantry and labourers. These millworkers may be divided into two classes : first, those who live at home and work in country mills ; next, those who have left home and are

employed in factories in towns or villages. Women working in
north of Ireland factories are miserably ill-paid, but when they
live with their relatives in the rural districts, their shilling or so
a day is often of service. Living in the country parts is cheap,
and girls belonging to a large family often find that working in
a mill to a certain extent "pays." In towns and villages, the
case is quite different; here there is rent to pay for the poor
habitation of the worker, she is separated from her family, and
either "boards" with someone, or clubs together with one or
two "hands" like herself. How far six shillings a-week will
go towards the support of full-grown, hard-worked girls in towns
and villages where living is as, or nearly as, dear as in England,
may be easily imagined. Some years ago, a correspondent of an
Irish newspaper [1] investigated the condition of some of the
Belfast millworkers, and described their mode of life. His description was that of a people whose condition could with difficulty be more miserable. The impression left on the editor's
mind after reading the account was that the millworkers would
be infinitely better lodged and more wholesomely fed in the
workhouse. Working-men are, as a rule, quite able to protect
their own interests, but the case is different with working-
women. Women living as these north of Ireland millworkers,
or, indeed, as women elsewhere in the British Isles, are injurious
to society if nothing else ; as the progeny of such ill-nourished
creatures must in time become a serious burden to the community. How far it would be possible for the State to enforce
a system of better housing and payment for those who are
unable to help themselves would not be easy to say. It might
be replied that the state of trade did not permit of better wages.
There might also be much talk about the laws of Political
Economy. As to these objections, the state of vulgar luxury in
which some of the proprietors, directors, and managers of these
factories live, might lead many to suppose that their profits
would allow of better wages being paid to the wretched beings

[1] Either *Freeman's Journal* or *Belfast Morning News.*

in their employment. As to the laws of Political Economy, the State has found it needful to interfere with these already, in order to protect the weak and helpless, and may find it necessary to do so again.

### (L, Page 118.)

The Irish fisherman has not been noticed in these pages. As he is in some cases a kind of peasant, and in others a sort of labourer, a short account of him may not be without interest.

There are on the Irish coast fishermen who go to sea in large boats, usually cutters, luggers, or a kind of sloop called a "hooker." There are also men who fish from open boats, and, as a consequence, do not go far out to sea. Some men belonging to both of these classes hold land in small quantities, and are farmers in springtime and later autumn. When their patches of grain and potatoes have been "put in," the owners go to sea in their own boats, if they have got any, and if not, they hire themselves out to "smack-owners." Many Irish fishermen hire themselves to Scotch smack-owners for the herring season. The editor has known of fishermen on the eastern and north-eastern coast leaving home when their fields or gardens have been planted and going to Scotland to be employed in the fishing season.

Though there are many smacks on the Irish coast, particularly on the eastern shore, they are not numerous enough to employ all the fishermen. The result is that the latter are obliged either to hire themselves on "foreign" smacks or to fish from open boats. These open boats are generally very roughly constructed, being usually built in or near the fishing villages by local builders. The cost is low, being often not more than a third of that charged by a regular boatbuilder at a seaport town. The editor has known of good eighteen and twenty feet boats being built for six or seven pounds. These appear very rudely constructed, but they are strong, and will "live" in very bad weather.

On the western and north-western coasts the canvas "curragh" or "corach" already described is used. Want of timber, and the great poverty of the people in those parts of Ireland, may account for such boats being still employed.

The want of large fishing smacks is a very serious one. Great loss of life is often caused by fishing from open boats, these being sometimes struck by squalls.

In the present spring two boats and several men were lost on the east coast, the casualty being altogether due to open boats.

Several reasons are put forward for the want of large-decked boats. One is the want of proper harbours in which such craft could take refuge. Now, unlike many parts of the English coast, there are numerous places along the shores of Ireland where harbours could be made at little cost, and where natural harbours could be improved. This, no doubt, has been done to some extent, but much remains to be done. There are many places where only open boats, which can be drawn up on the shore, are kept, simply because a harbour has not been improved or deepened, or a pier already made not kept up. The accident just named took place a few miles from a little port, whose pier was partly washed away a few years ago. The harbour is now useless, and fishing is carried on from open boats. As mountains, nearly three thousand feet in height, rise abruptly from the coast, the squalls, with certain winds, are very dangerous, and casualties have been very common. Yet nothing has been done for years past to repair the little pier. Different persons, public and private, are blamed for this neglect, and it is a difficult matter to find out where the fault lies. The fact remains, that last autumn the pier was in its ruinous state daily becoming worse, and that nothing had been done towards repairing it. Without proper piers and harbours it is not to be expected that anyone will embark capital in building fishing smacks, and loss of life and of money is the result.

No doubt, on the other hand it may be said, that where there are good harbours, "foreigners," *i.e.*, Cornish, Manx, and Scotch fishermen get most of the fish, and that Irish fishermen are behind-hand. There is, no doubt, some truth in this, but the fault would seem to lie with persons other than the fishermen, as the latter are so numerous and willing to work that they hire themselves in Scotch boats. There seems a great indisposition on the part of persons with capital in Ireland to embark it in any sort of maritime enterprise, such as smack-owning would be. Although there is plenty of capital in and around Dublin, and in parts of Ulster, and many good harbours are to be found in those parts of Ireland, yet smack-owners are few. This want of enterprise is a serious drawback to Ireland, as it means a very heavy annual loss to the country. And whatever may be said in favour of State assistance to buy boats along the far western shores of Ireland, where aid of some kind is sorely needed, there is certainly no necessity for such in the east or north of Ireland.

As a rule the fishermen are very poor : they are a poor class everywhere, but particularly so in Ireland. The only exceptions to the rule are in those instances where the fishermen are small farmers as well. In many cases within the editor's knowledge, where men have had a few acres of good land, and were in the habit of hiring in smacks during the herring season, they have been in comfortable circumstances. There may be seen in some places snug cottages belonging to such men, these being often surrounded by flower gardens. The explanation given for the very unusual sight of flowers in rural Ireland is, that "The women manage the farms whilst the men are away at the fishing, and that women always like flowers about a place." Fishermen of this stamp are unfortunately few in number, being limited very much, so far as the editor is aware, to one district. It is much to be desired that the number of such men could be increased. This can only be done by the public authorities improving the harbours, and by private persons showing a greater spirit of enterprise.

### (M, Page 147.)

The editor cannot hold himself responsible for the exact truthfulness of everything stated in the preceding pages. Everything is accurate so far as he knows, and where the facts have not been within his personal knowledge, they have been verified as far as possible by reference to the best possible sources of information. What have been herein stated as facts are to be taken as generally true, but, as exceptions may be found to every rule, not universally true.

www.ingramcontent.com/pod-product-compliance
Lightning Source LLC
Chambersburg PA
CBHW020544270326
41927CB00006B/714